UNDERSTANDING

CYNTHIA OZICK

Understanding Contemporary American Literature

Matthew J. Bruccoli, *Editor*

UNDERSTANDING
Cynthia
OZICK

LAWRENCE S. FRIEDMAN

UNIVERSITY OF SOUTH CAROLINA PRESS

Copyright © 1991 University of South Carolina

Published in Columbia, South Carolina,
by the University of South Carolina Press

Manufactured in the United States of America

Library of Congress Cataloging-in-Publication Data

Friedman, Lawrence S.
    Understanding Cynthia Ozick / Lawrence S. Friedman.
       p.   cm. — (Understanding contemporary American literature)
    Includes bibliographical references and index.
    ISBN 0-87249-772-0
    1.Ozick, Cynthia—Criticisim and interpretation.   I.Title.
    II.Series.
    PS3565.Z5Z65   1991
    813'.54—dc20   91–14081

CONTENTS

EDITOR'S PREFACE

Understanding Contemporary American Literature has been planned as a series of guides or companions for students as well as good nonacademic readers. The editor and publisher perceive a need for these volumes because much of the influential contemporary literature makes special demands. Uninitiated readers encounter difficulty in approaching works that depart from the traditional forms and techniques of prose and poetry. Literature relies on conventions, but the conventions keep evolving; new writers form their own conventions—which in time may become familiar. Put simply, *UCAL* provides instruction in how to read certain contemporary writers—identifying and explicating their material, themes, use of language, point of view, structures, symbolism, and responses to experience.

The word *understanding* in the series title was deliberately chosen. Many willing readers lack an adequate understanding of how contemporary literature works; that is, what the author is attempting to express and the means by which it is conveyed. Although the criticism and analysis in the series have been aimed at a level of general accessibility, these introductory volumes are meant to be applied in conjunction with the works they cover. Thus they do not provide a substitute for the works and authors they introduce, but rather prepare the reader for more profitable literary experiences.

M. J. B.

UNDERSTANDING
CYNTHIA OZICK

CHAPTER ONE

Understanding Cynthia Ozick

Career

Cynthia Ozick is a native New Yorker whose Russian Jewish immigrant parents encountered American life for the first time on the Lower East Side of Manhattan. Born in 1928, she grew up in the Pelham Bay section of the Bronx, where her parents had escaped the Lower East Side just as her generation would desert the Bronx for the suburbs. Nostalgia for the Bronx—home to lost parents, vanished childhood, dispersed Jewish community— washes periodically over Ruth Puttermesser, heroine of two stories in *Levitation: Five Fictions* (1982). A some-time Ozick alter ego, Puttermesser shares with her creator not only Bronx memories but the love for chocolate that Ozick probably acquired amidst the sweets in her parents' Park View Pharmacy. Like Bernard Malamud, whose story "The Silver Crown" figures prominently in her "Usurpation (Other People's Stories)" [*Bloodshed and Three Novellas,* 1976], Ozick writes most frequently about Jews in contemporary New York. Her own Jewishness was impressed upon her by the anti-Semitism she experienced in the neighborhood and at school, P.S. 71, where she was "publicly shamed" and "repeatedly accused of deicide" for failing to sing Christmas carols in assembly. During the school day she felt "friendless and forlorn"; but in the Park View Pharmacy "in the winter dusk" she was transported by books borrowed from the Traveling Library. Ozick traces her desire to write back to the "bliss" of early reading and beyond: "Even at age 6—no, as soon as I was conscious of being alive—I knew I was a writer." She may also have been inspired by the example of her mother's brother, Abraham Regelson, a Zionist, a Hebrew poet, and "a kind of spiritual model. So by the time I left P.S. 71 and went to Hunter High School, my being a writer was an old fact about myself."[1]

Although she had attended *cheder* (religious school) as well as P.S. 71, Ozick claims to have learned nothing from her childhood Hebrew studies. The rich lode of Jewish learning that runs through her writing was discovered by a self-described "Jewish autodidact." Puttermesser's Hebrew lessons and imaginative resurrection of a dead Uncle Zindel and his apocryphal East European ghetto reflect Ozick's deepening immersion in the traditional Judaism which she had taken for granted as a child. But at Hunter High School she instead became enthralled with the Latin poets. An unpublished volume of poetry, "Greeks and Jews," is included among her works, and several of her translations appear in *A Treasury of Yiddish Poetry* (ed. Irving Howe and Eleizer Greenberg, 1969). The title "Greeks and Jews" announces the Hellenism versus Hebraism theme that features so prominently in Ozick's fiction. Much of the dramatic tension of her stories arises from the clash between these disparate belief systems, the former characterized by polytheism, the latter by monotheism. The transcendent embodiment of the Jewish idea, monotheism stands opposed to a variety of heresies ranging from Canaanite idols to Freudian psychology. As emblazoned in the strictures of the Second Commandment monotheism automatically evokes Jewish allegiance. Because monotheism therefore serves as a litmus test of Jewish authenticity, a crucial concern of Ozick's, it is rarely absent from her fiction and essays.

After Hunter High School Ozick went to New York University. Nearly forty years later she recalled the "colorless February morning in 1946" when she first took the subway downtown to Washington Square.[2] To the seventeen-and-a-half-year-old girl ("carrying my lunch in a brown paper bag just as I had carried it to high school only a month before") Washington Square even in gray February "had the allure of the celestial unknown." Life was "luminously new: I felt my youth like a nimbus." A day early for the beginning of classes, Ozick was struck, at least in retrospect, by all she doesn't know: the "gods" who publish in *Partisan Review;* the house on the north side of the Square where Henry James was born; the nearby dwelling places of W. H. Auden and Marianne Moore. Later that same February she bought her first "real" book ("not for the classroom")—Thomas Wolfe's *Of Time and the River*—which for weeks she had been coveting. Soon Ozick is one of "the sorrowful literary young" haunting secondhand bookshops, her future course already apparent. Although she went on to graduate school after New York University, her ambitions were already more literary than scholarly.

At Ohio State University she wrote a 1950 master's thesis entitled "Parable in the Late Novels of Henry James" on the author who would most influence her own writing.

That influence was nearly fatal for the young Ozick, whose obsession with living up to the moral and artistic ideals of James which so attracted her imposed too heavy a burden on her fledgling talent. In a 1982 essay, ''The Lesson of the Master,'' Ozick bemoans the many months she sat cramped in a ''bleak microfilm cell'' writing her thesis while James was ''despoiling'' her youth. Reading James's ''The Beast in the Jungle,'' the young Ozick saw herself in the story's protagonist, John Marcher, who imagines himself earmarked for a special but unknown fate which he endlessly—and ultimately, futilely—awaits. For Ozick manifest destiny lay in awaiting, equally futilely, ''the ambush of sacred and sublime literature'' which would instantaneously confer upon her the ability to produce Jamesian masterpieces. ''Leaving graduate school at the age of twenty-two, disdaining the Ph.D. as an acquisition surely beneath the concerns of literary seriousness, I was,'' recalls Ozick, ''already Henry James.''[3] Even if one could at twenty-two hope to emulate the master, it is solely amidst James's own apprentice work that attainable models may be found. ''Influence,'' concludes Ozick, ''is perdition.''

The influence of James cost Ozick her youth. Looking back more than twenty years later, she regrets the years wasted in attempting a ''philosophical'' novel called ''Mercy, Pity, Peace, and Love'': ''If I were twenty-two now, I would not undertake a cannibalistically Jamesian novel to begin with.''[4] This seven-year period of ''madness'' spent in pursuit of the ''ferocious dream'' of writing a masterpiece on the order of James's *The Ambassadors* Ozick calls ''my mournful, miserable start, which was a nonstart.''[5] Six and a half more years would pass between the desertion of ''Mercy, Pity, Peace, and

Love'' and the completion of *Trust*—on the day of John F. Kennedy's assassination. *Trust* (1966), a novel every bit as massive as its abandoned predecessor, remains an anomaly among Ozick's fiction, the last "extended immolation" she would endure. After *Trust,* Ozick needed "quick spurts of immediacy" and began writing short stories "which could get published right away." But "the stories too took years and years to find publication and some recognition." As late as 1982 she still considered herself a "hopeful tyro" since no matter what she submitted—verse, fiction, nonfiction—it "had to battle for publication." This constant struggle left her literary psyche permanently scarred: "I have never recovered from early neglect. Who does?"[6]

In Ozick's case the vagaries of publication proved especially disturbing. A slow and meticulous composer, she became fearful of again investing the many years it would take her to write another long novel. In a 1985 essay, "The Seam of the Snail," Ozick calls herself a "pinched perfectionist" who attempts the next sentence only when she is satisfied that its predecessor is as nearly flawless as she can make it. Because "nothing matters" to her "so much as a comely and muscular sentence," she burnishes her prose endlessly, wearing herself away "while making scarcely any progress at all." In her torturous habit of composition she resembles the snail: "I measure my life in sentences pressed out, line by line, like the lustrous ooze on the underside of the snail, the snail's secret open seam, its wound, leaking attar."[7] Such evident belief in the sanctity of words may account in part for the style— "every paragraph a poem"—of *Trust.* Her subsequent radical shift in literary strategy reflects weariness with the stylistic demands of a fiction that aspires to the "High

Art'' of Henry James or E. M. Forster. As a deeply committed Jew, however, Ozick retains her religious reverence for words even as she abandons the art novel for the short story and the novella. Even in *Trust,* a novel reflecting her philosophical and social concerns in the 1950s, Jewish words oppose pagan idols; and Ozick's transcendent theme—the ramifications of Jewish identity—snaps into focus at the end.

With the publication of her first volume of short fiction, *The Pagan Rabbi and Other Stories* (1971), Judaism is firmly established as the dominant force in Ozick's work. Not only the "mandarin" style but the Gentile cultural nexus of *Trust* has been abandoned. The primary focus of the seven stories in *The Pagan Rabbi* is maintained in the succeeding collections—*Bloodshed and Three Novellas* (1976) and *Levitation: Five Fictions* (1982). All three title stories, for example, test Jewish belief, relating authentic Jewishness in one way or another to the willing assumption of the burdens of Jewish history, most notably that of the Holocaust. While her stories dealing with what it means to be Jewish understandably fail to achieve broad popular success, they have earned wide critical acclaim. Ozick has won some dozen literary awards, including the B'nai B'rith Jewish Heritage Award (1971); the Edward Wallant Memorial Award (1972); the Jewish Book Council Award for Fiction (1972); the American Academy Award (1973); and several O. Henry Awards (1975, 1981, 1984). Perhaps the most prestigious, not to say the most lucrative, recognition accorded Ozick was her 1983 selection as one of the first two recipients of the American Academy and Institute of Arts and Letters' Mildred and Harold Strauss Livings. This tax-free grant ($35,000 a year for a minimum of five years in Ozick's case) is designed to enable writers to concentrate full-time on their writing. No longer could Ozick joke about being "on a Hallote"—she is married to attorney Bernard Hallote and lives with him and their daughter in Yonkers, a suburb of New York City—by way of explaining her means of support.

After the success of her three volumes of short fiction Ozick turned once again to the novel, treating in *The Cannibal Galaxy* (1983) the spiritual struggles of a Holocaust survivor who becomes headmaster of a school in the American Midwest. *The Messiah of Stockholm* (1987), a novella, likewise explores the issue of Jewish identity, this time by relating it to questions of literary authorship. A wholly imaginative premise—the discovery of a lost manuscript attributed to the Polish Jewish writer Bruno Schulz, killed by the Nazis in 1942—becomes the springboard for raising questions about authenticity that transcend the purely literary. Still, both *The Cannibal Galaxy* and *The Messiah of Stockholm* reflect Ozick's vow to keep her fiction short. "I don't think I'll write another big novel. I'm afraid to. I don't have 14 years to throw out like that anymore."[8] What seems most valuable about her writing, however, derives less from its form than from its content. Stories, novels, and essays—more than fifty of which are collected in *Art and Ardor* (1983) and *Metaphor and Memory* (1989)—alike reflect the deep moral seriousness that leads Ozick to revise the modernist aesthetic and proclaim in the preface to *Bloodshed* that "a story must not merely *be,* but mean."

Overview

"I believe that stories ought to judge and interpret the world," Cynthia Ozick wrote in the *Bloodshed* preface. Hers is therefore a moral fiction, set in a world in which human actions matter. A passionate advocate of an essentially Jewish literature which, although written in English, she calls "liturgical," Ozick observes the world through the eyes of a deeply committed Jew. Opposing ideologies clash on the moral battleground of fictions peopled largely by contemporary Jews. On one side is covenantal Judaism; on the other, whatever is not: paganism, Christianity, secularism. A quintessential Ozick story, "The Pagan Rabbi" forces the title character, Isaac Kornfeld, to choose between Jewish and pagan values embodied respectively in his first and last names. Although it is Hellenism that here constitutes the opposing ideology, it might just as well be any system that inculcates multiplicity. Because Judaism is above all monotheistic, the Jew must shun idolatry in all its many forms and hew steadfastly to the Second Commandment. In a typical Ozick story idol worship signifies moral transgression. And if one of her Jews strays from the path of righteousness, his apostasy generally consists of abandoning one God for many gods. Uncompromisingly monotheistic, Judaism (and Ozick) refuses to countenance divided allegiance. What initially appear to be arbitrary or misconceived antitheses to Jewishness—nature in "The Pagan Rabbi"; art in "Usurpation (Other People's Stories)"; Christianity in "Levitation"—invariably turn into idolatrous systems rooted in polytheism and thus radically opposed to the Jewish idea. So pure for Ozick is this idea that it threatens to undermine its artistic expression. Since art itself can be the locus of competing ideologies, the Jewish writer must endlessly confront the dilemma not only of what to write but of whether to write at all. In the same preface to *Bloodshed*—one of her most important aesthetic statements—that reveals her moral intentions, Ozick also expresses her anxieties as a Jewish writer. As she wrestles to overcome her fear that fiction is at best frivolous, at worst idolatrous, she is uncertain even about the language in which she writes. Because "English is a Christian language," it may prove inadequate to communicate Jewish experience. The moral struggle at the heart of Ozick's art reflects her struggle to embody the Jewish idea in fictional form.

"All that is not law is levity," the lesson for story writers in "Usurpation (Other People's Stories)," applies equally to any but holy writing. When Ozick calls the preface to *Bloodshed* "a piece of fiction like any other," she conflates genres not so much to obliterate the distinction between fiction and nonfiction as to call attention to their shared attributes.[9] To judge and interpret the world must be the ideal of the essayist as well as the story writer. Many of Ozick's essays in *Art and Ardor* and *Metaphor and Memory* reflect in theoretical, often polemical, form the same moral and aesthetic concerns that surface in her fiction. Because her writing is so deeply rooted in Jewishness, those essays which trace the contours of Jewish belief loom large. "America: Toward Yavneh" (1970), for example, contains, among other things, fragments of an intellectual autobiography. While its overarching purpose is to call for a "liturgical" literature conceived in ethics rather than aesthetics and written in Judaized English, the essay simultaneously chronicles Ozick's moral development. Art—"the religion of the Gentile nations"—had so dominated her life that she "had no other aspiration, no other commitment, was zealous for no other creed."[10] *Trust,* written under the spell of Henry James and E. M. Forster and reflecting their single-minded dedication to the "Work of Art," was therefore begun ''for the Gentiles'' though finished for the Jews. In the return of Enoch Vand, the novel's only Jew, to convenantal Judaism, Ozick discovers her character and theme. Vand's ''conversion''—and Ozick's—is triggered by a rejection of the values of the surrounding culture, a revulsion against Western Civilization itself. Assimilation is anathema, involving as it does the yielding up of Jewish identity, the homogenization of Jewish uniqueness. Because assimilation is tantamount to surrender, surrender to disappearance, the Jewish writer must resist aping Gentile culture. Rather than efface their own culture by servile imitation, Jews should preserve it ''by bursting forth with a literature attentive to the implications of Covenant and Commandment.''[11]

These implications reached Ozick via Rabbi Leo Baeck's ''Romantic Religion,'' an essay which powerfully influenced her thought. Originally published in 1922 but revised and greatly expanded in 1938, the essay sharpens the distinction between Christianity—romantic religion—and Judaism—classical religion—to the advantage of the latter. Ozick's linkage—and distrust—of romance, imagination, and Christianity, already announced by *Trust*'s Enoch Vand even before his re-Judaization, originates in Baeck. Christianity, according to Baeck, surrenders to the mood of helplessness by withdrawing from the world and retreating into the past, thereby destroying ethics. Like all romantic religions it ''seeks its goals in the now mythical, now mystical visions of the imagination. Its world is the realm in which all rules are suspended in the remote which transcends all things.''[12] Rooted in revelation—a moment of grace and redemption unrelated to man's striving in which reception becomes fulfillment—Christianity negates the ethical action at the heart of Judaism. In Judaism, a classical religion, man attains freedom via the commandment, not, as in romantic religion, via grace. Salvation, conferred as a gift upon passive Christians, must be fought for actively by Jews. Christianity, which already has its Messiah, is a "finished" religion, its central event long past and the locus of sentimental longing. Longing, "a mere mood" in romantic religions, strives in classical religions such as Judaism "to unify all men and impels them to follow the commandment of God."[13] Ozick follows Baeck in regarding romanticism as an enemy confronted in all walks of life. What Baeck attacks as subservience to the Nazi state in 1938 Germany characterizes romantic religion's coming to terms with tyrants, a phenomenon Enoch Vand spots in Christianity's rendering the world unto Caesar. In light of Baeck's view that the romantic mood was most at home in Germany, the rise of Nazism comes as no surprise to those who read the Holocaust as the ultimate explosion of the romantic imagination at its most aberrant. Such a reading may explain Ozick's otherwise bizarre choice of a quotation from Joseph Goebbels, the infamous Nazi propagandist, to the effect that men seek to force the world to conform to the pattern of their inner lives as an epigraph to "A Mercenary" (*Bloodshed and Three Novellas*). That the Nazis were far from oblivious to the political implications of Baeck's "Romantic Religion" is evident in their immediate confiscation and destruction of the 1938 collection in which the essay appeared.

Against romance Baeck—and Ozick—invokes history. And Judaism in celebrating that holiness which arises from ethical responses to the concrete realities of life (i.e., history) stands opposed to romantic religions which incarnate holiness in the dreams and longing that symptomize withdrawal from the world. Ethical action, the lifeblood of Judaism, is powerfully dramatized by Ozick in "Puttermesser and Xanthippe," the novella that concludes *Levitation: Five Fictions*. Puttermesser, representing the Jewish tradition (she studies Hebrew, reads holy texts) and its ideal of service (she works for the city at a fraction of the salary she can—and did—command as a corporate lawyer), cleans up New York, transforming it temporarily into a "city of seraphim" during her brief reign as mayor. Herself a dreamer, Puttermesser nonetheless refuses to allow private fantasy to overwhelm rational purpose. The Puttermesser who studies Hebrew, invents Jewish forebears and their representative *shtetl,* and clings to the apartment in the crumbling formerly Jewish neighborhood where she grew up, is a recurring character type in Ozick's fiction. Invariably Jews, such characters resist those who would efface the past, realizing that only in the facts of history is Jewish culture, all but wiped out in the Holocaust, preserved. Enoch Vand tabulates death camp victims (*Trust*); Edelshtein seeks a translator who will preserve in English his Yiddish poems that memorialize Jewish tradition but exist only in a dying language ("Envy; or Yiddish in America"); Genevieve forces the Holocaust back into collective memory ("The Suitcase"); and Lushinski prods his mistress to read Raul Hilberg's *The Destruction of the European Jews* and Elie Wiesel's *Night* ("A Mercenary"). A good deal of Ozick's moral drama derives from confrontations between Jews who invoke history and Gentiles (occasionally Jews) who prefer to forget it. Allegra Vand (*Trust*), Hannah ("Envy"), Mr. Hencke ("The Suitcase"), and Lulu ("A Mercenary") cannot un-

derstand the compulsion to remember. "Genevieve in-
vokes History always," disapprovingly remarks Mr.
Hencke, still the uneasy German some twenty years after
World War II.

The historical imperative to remember is a crucial aspect of Jewish solidarity. Acts of witnessing and recording
symbolically restore Holocaust losses in reconstituting the
vanished Jewish community. Ozick's "centrally Jewish"
writing is liturgical in that it commands the "reciprocal
moral imagination" rather than "the isolated lyrical
imagination." It is "a choral voice, a communal voice:
the echo of the voice of the Lord of History,"[14] Historical
awareness is an indispensable component of Jewish identity in fictions that relentlessly draw the line between the
authentic and the false. The many appeals to history in
Ozick's stories also testify to Jewish textuality. Because
Judaism is a religion of the Word—as incarnated most en-
duringly in the Ten Commandments—it is little wonder
that authentic Jews rely upon words—as incarnated, for
example, in historical as well as in holy texts—to ensure
their communal survival. Words and the texts that contain
them are particularly indispensable to a religion that for-
bids traffic in images, a religion whose God *"cannot,
may not, be physically imagined."*[15] Idolatry, a sure sign
of Jewish inauthenticity, is interpreted by Ozick to mean
not only the worship of material objects or images but of
anything that threatens to violate the strictures of the Second Commandment. In "From a Refugee's Notebook"
the many "stone godlets" crowding Freud's room distance the nominally Jewish father of psychoanalysis from
the religion of his forebears. A less obvious but more pervasive strategy for signaling Jewishness is Ozick's equation of idolatry and art. In the *Bloodshed* preface she calls

"Usurpation (Other People's Stories)" "a story written against story-writing, . . . an invention directed against inventing—the point being that the story-making faculty itself can be a corridor to the corruptions and abominations of idol-worship." Several of her essays reflect the same "dread of the imagination" and consequent unease about the artistic enterprise that surfaces in "Usurpation." In the revealingly titled "Literature as Idol: Harold Bloom" Ozick, having acknowledged the strong Jewish elements in Bloom's work, takes the literary scholar to task for erecting "an artistic anti-Judaism." Bloom is an idol-maker, poems his idols. Like all idol-makers he "envies the Creator, hopes to compete with the Creator, and schemes to invent a substitute for the Creator."[16] Ozick herself regards imaginative literature as an idol but one with which "we are safe" as long as we recognize it as essentially a plaything. If, however, like Bloom, we make of it a "self-contained magic system," then literature becomes willy-nilly an object of worship in violation of the Second Commandment. Like any serious Jewish writer Ozick is subject to the tension created by the sometimes antithetical demands of religion and art. To be a writer is to risk competing with the Creator, thereby drawing perilously close to what the Jew must shun: "The strivings of divination—i.e., of God-competition—lead away from the Second Commandment, ultimately contradict it."[17]

Bloom's idea that the "making that is poetry is god-making" forges a link between the work of art and pagan theology. The fear that those who make art serve pagan gods instead of the Jewish God threads through Ozick's writing. Yet nature is as suspect as art. Because the pagan gods are "the spontaneous gods of nature," Jews must resist the siren song of the natural world that lures Isaac

Kornfeld to his doom in "The Pagan Rabbi." A recurring motif in Ozick's fiction is the opposition of pagan naturalism to Jewish traditional religious practice. Given her repeated warning that the "God of the Jews must not be conceived of as belonging to nature," it follows that the nature-worshiping rabbi forfeits all claim to Jewish authenticity. His paganization and subsequent spiritual death takes the form of forsaking his wife Sheindel (Judaism) for a tree nymph (Nature). Variations on the same theme occur in *Trust,* where Nick Tilbeck exalts nature, Enoch Vand, history; in "Usurpation," where Tchernikhovsky's poems are profane, Agnon's stories holy; and in "Levitation," where Lucy the Christian is married to Feingold the Jew. "The Butterfly and the Traffic Light," one of Ozick's earliest stories, dramatizes the clash between opposing belief systems that animates so much of her fiction. Fishbein calls Isabel's opinion that an advanced religion is monotheistic (Judaism) foolish, comparing her fixation on one God to a fixation on one idea and adding that the ancients had a "god for every personality," the Church "a saint for every mood." And when Lucy, a Jewish convert, reverts to Christianity in "Levitation," she perceives the eternal as a continuum stretching from the Madonna back through Venus and Aphrodite to Astarte. Although Ozick lumps Christianity together with paganism as essentially polytheistic, she generally locates in Hellenism those beliefs antithetical to Judaism. In her fiction the Hellenism that spawned pagan gods repeatedly squares off against the Hebraism that invented monotheism. The battle between conflicting values is fought in the hearts and minds of Ozick's Jewish protagonists, many of whom share her early fascination with Hellenism but all of whom can attain, maintain, or regain moral stature only in fidelity to Judaism. Two of her most powerful stories respectively illustrate the surrender to, and the overcoming of, pagan temptations associated with the Hellenic world. In "The Pagan Rabbi," Isaac Kornfeld's nature worship culminates in suicide; in "Usurpation" the narrator is saved by her last-minute deflection from the worship of art. Significantly, Jewish prayer implements play decisive roles in both stories: the rabbi hangs himself in his prayer shawl; the narrator is bound to Judaism by phylacteries.

While Jewish identity may be defined or clarified in the opposition to paganism, Ozick's central theme may be expressed equally powerfully, if less overtly, by internalizing moral conflict. Lushinski, the acculturated and cosmopolitan Jew of "A Mercenary" and a man of many identities, claims to be part of mankind. Still, he is ultimately overtaken by memories of his Jewish past from which he endlessly flees but cannot entirely escape. A Jew *malgré lui,* he achieves a certain authenticity by virtue of his inability to forget. A similarly provisional Jewish identity is conferred upon Bleilip, another acculturated Jew, by the rebbe at the end of "Bloodshed." Surrounded by pious Jews, Bleilip hears in their Yiddish the accents of his dead grandfather, the echos of a Jewish past. Forced by the holy rebbe to confront the spiritual emptiness of his "secularist" life, Bleilip shows signs of turning back to the faith he had abandoned. In both novellas Jewish identity is largely determined by historical awareness centering on the Holocaust: Lushinski is a Holocaust survivor as are the Hasidim and their rebbe. And in "Levitation" the authentic Jews who gather about a Holocaust survivor rise toward the ceiling while the inauthentic Jews in another room remain firmly anchored to the floor. *The Shawl*

(1989), Ozick's most direct evocation of the Holocaust, makes it clear that all Jews, even death camp survivors, owe a debt to their coreligionists. To abandon Jewishness in the agony of despair may be psychologically understandable but morally indefensible. More obviously than any other Ozick fiction, *The Shawl* couples Jewish identity with fidelity to the Jewish past as incarnated by Holocaust remembrance. Yet Rosa, its central character, dilutes her Jewishness not by failing to remember the past but by falsifying it. Sanctifying her murdered baby, Rosa refashions a past she can live in, a haven from the atrocities of the real past and from the bitterness of a hellish present. Her value as a Jew, however, is made contingent upon abandoning romantic fiction for historical fact.

Any American Jewish writer who treats the Holocaust approaches the limits of artistic representation. To fictionalize is to trivialize, argue many, notably the German refugee philosopher T. W. Adorno, who bitterly—and unequivocally—stated that such an all-consuming tragedy must remain outside the province of art where "it is transfigured and stripped of some of its horror and with this, injustice is already done to the victims."[18] Others, no less conscious of the moral and aesthetic risks of representing the Holocaust, argue that words, fictional as well as factual, forge links between the living and the dead and, albeit imperfectly, memorialize the vanished Jewish millions. American Jewish writers conscious also of their relative distance—psychological as well as geographical—from the European victims, generally represent the Holocaust indirectly. Saul Bellow's *The Victim,* for example, may be read as an allegory of the Holocaust in which Leventhal, the quintessential Jew, endures the "persecution" of the significantly named anti-Semite, Allbee. Less indirect and more typical of American Jewish Holocaust fiction is *Mr. Sammler's Planet,* a Bellow novel whose protagonist is a seventy-year-old survivor who lost a wife and an eye. Although *The Shawl* opens in a Nazi concentration camp, it, like *Mr. Sammler's Planet* and other important postwar American Jewish fiction such as Edward Wallant's *The Pawnbroker* and Isaac Bashevis Singer's *Enemies, a Love Story,* focuses on Holocaust survivors in the United States. Joseph Brill, the central character of *The Cannibal Galaxy,* is Ozick's fullest treatment of a Holocaust survivor. Along with Rosa, Mr. Sammler, Wallant's Sol Nazerman, and Singer's Herman Broder, Brill embodies the trauma of survivors who find it all but impossible to justify, much less to validate, post-Holocaust existence. Common to them all is the certainty that "real" life ended in Europe; what life persists in America is merely endured, impossible to enjoy.

Confronting the Holocaust is nearly inevitable for writers whose aim is to invoke Jewish experience. So mountainously does the Holocaust loom up in modern Jewish history that the fear of representing it collides with the fear that failing to represent it is to misrepresent Jewish experience. Paradoxically, the deeper the commitment to Judaism, the sharper the horns of the dilemma. Thus Ozick's fear that story writing violates the Second Commandment's strictures against idolatry is exacerbated by doubts about fictionalizing the Holocaust in the first place. Her decision to publish *The Shawl* in book form years after its two stories had appeared separately in *The New Yorker* may reflect her struggle with, and ultimate resolution of, the problem of Holocaust representation. To be sure, Ozick's goal of expressing the "Jewish Idea" remains steadfast; but her 1983 essay "Bialik's Hint" modifies the expressive strategies announced in "Toward a

New Yiddish'' some thirteen years earlier. No longer does
she embrace her ''old fantasy of New Yiddish—i.e. the
Judaization of a single language used by large populations
of Jews.'' Although she welcomes the enrichment of an
English infused by Jewish concepts, she has abandoned
''any theory of an indispensable language.''[19] Not only is
''New Yiddish'' irrelevant, but ''a saving midrashic
form'' is inadequate for a genuine Jewish literature. Yet
the tradition of midrash (exposition, explanation) seasons
the ''purely imaginative'' with ''the elements of judgment
and interpretation'' that Ozick deems indispensable to
such a literature. Midrashic form should therefore be re-
tained as a means, if not *the* means, of expressing the
Jewish idea. Since an entire literature can be grounded
neither in a single form (midrashim) nor in a single language (New Yiddish), Ozick seizes upon Bialik's hint—
''the fusion of the offerings of the Enlightenment . . .
with Jewish primacy''—as a new strategy for expressing
Jewish moral seriousness.

Chaim Nachman Bialik's was a ''post-Enlightenment
mentality . . . engaged in a modernist literary contempla-
tion'' that produced a ''fusion of secular aesthetic culture
with Jewish sensibility.''[20] His turn-of-the-century rendez-
vous with Enlightenment ideology foreshadows the post-
Holocaust encounter with modernism. The foremost
Jewish poet of his day and the fount of Hebrew modernism, Bialik wrote at a time when the spread of secular
values threatened to erode traditional religious beliefs. ''In
the City of Slaughter'' (1905) responds to catastrophe ''by
retaining the familiar symbols and constructs yet altering
their context and significance, . . . conveying the ambiguities and complexities of a new spiritual reality.''[21] Bialik's poem incarnates Ozick's call for a liturgical writing,
hinting at a methodology she will make her own. Refusing

unconditional surrender to Enlightenment values (which presages future assimilation), Bialik instead grafts them onto the Jewish language of moral seriousness and collective conscience. Dedicated to achieving a comparable fusion, Ozick must confront secular challenges infinitely stronger than those Bialik faced. The half century and more since Bialik wrote has witnessed equally irreversible Jewish losses and secular gains. For Ozick to emulate Bialik in her stated aim of writing stories that "judge and interpret the world," she is forced to reject most of the moral and many of the aesthetic principles of the twentieth century. While her Hebraism versus Hellenism formula encodes both moral and aesthetic positions, the latter must also be examined within the context of Ozick's love-hate affair with literary modernism.

What Ozick values most in modernism is its moral seriousness, as embodied in the "High Art" of Henry James. Although James presides over her fiction, especially *Trust*—"a cannibalistically Jamesian novel"—she has also cited Forster, Chekhov, Conrad, and Hardy as authors who "intimately and obsessively" influenced various stages of her work. Reading Hardy, for example, she encounters "life observed and understood as well as felt" by a writer whose ability "to penetrate into the whole lives of human beings" is grounded in his "knowledge of something real, something *there*."[22] That art which is most interesting and lasting is, like Hardy's, didactic, teaching "what it means to be a human being." Lacking the "corona of moral purpose" that envelops Hardy's fiction, literature is without meaning. And without meaning, art becomes its own raison d'être, akin to those idols Ozick and all Jews abhor. *"What literature means is meaning,"* insists Ozick; and because *"Literature is for*

the sake of humanity'' rather than for its own sake, meaning resides not in the idols of imagination or language but
in the reality of experience: *"Literature is the recognition
of the particular.''*[23] Ozick invokes the moral fiction of
the great modernists in her own by reaffirming their emphasis on the importance of subject matter. To maintain
that subjects are interchangeable is to deny the
distinction-making capacity that empowers moral art. The
creators of that art were, says Ozick, as "magisterial" as
their works. What Hardy "knew"—and could embody in
his fiction—rested upon self-knowledge. Like James and
the other giants of literary modernism, he knew himself
as the "Sublime and Magisterial Artist." While Ozick admits that it cannot (and probably should not) be recovered, this concept of the artist engendered "masterly
confidence." In the artist's individuality lay the consistent
moral vision of his art. Ozick is able to express an equally
consistent moral vision by housing her muse not in herself
but in Jewishness.

It is of course her Jewishness that distinguishes Ozick
from other postmodernists, including most Jews. Philip
Roth, for one, creates in *The Counterlife* characters "so
wilily infiltrated by postmodernist inconstancy that they
keep revising their speeches and their fates: you can't
trust them even to stay dead.''[24] While it is not necessary
to believe that he is as "anxiously protean" as his characters, the moral confidence that James finds in himself
and that Ozick finds in Jewishness eludes Roth. Of course
Roth may not be interested in consistency, moral or otherwise; nor may he care about Ozick's aim to judge and
interpret the world. Since, however, his muse remains
houseless, Roth's fiction seems not to express "the writer's relationship to a set of ideas, or to the universe" that

for Ozick is crucial to literature. Finding her own viable matrix of ideas in Judaism, Ozick is liberated from the tyranny of the subjective self and empowered to create the serious art that arises "from the amazing permutations of the objective world." So leery is she of artistic subjectivism that even E. M. Forster—formerly among the most secure in Ozick's pantheon of modern masters—"has grown thinner" for her after the publication of *Maurice* (1971). Forster's single overtly homosexual novel, *Maurice* is "an infantile book, because, while pretending to be about societal injustice, it is really about make-believe, it is about wishing; so it fails even as a tract." A "daydream without pictures," *Maurice* represents a failure of nerve; its softness results from Forster's tiptoeing around its homosexual theme instead of portraying it concretely. The novel is ultimately no more than a display of its author's wounded psyche, a novel which makes it "clear that Forster's famous humanism is a kind of personal withdrawal rather than a universal testimony, and reverberates with despair."[25] Like postmodern self-reflexive fiction *Maurice* valorizes the artist's persona at the expense of factual subject matter. It is akin to that fiction which claims to be about "the language it is made out of." To the extent that its actual subject is either its author or its language, all such self-referential art negates the "nimbus of *meaning*" that for Ozick validates its creation.[26]

That fiction which is about itself is a poem without a history, which is to say an idol. Whether its specific idol is author or text, it aims to be self-sustaining, thus incarnating an aesthetic that is alien to Jewish belief. The writer who "wants to stay Jewish" cannot subscribe to the "religion of Art." Necessarily indifferent to its enclosed aesthetic, the Jew wants "to passionately wallow in the human reality."[27] And because for Ozick human reality consists of more than the sum total of individual egos, she dislikes Forster's world "where personal relationships govern . . . and there are no communal contracts." Dealing as it must with covenant and conduct, the Jewish literature that Ozick envisions—and practices—speaks with a "communal voice." The nineteenth-century novel, pronounced dead by many postmodern critics, remains a truer model for Jewish writers than the host of self-referential fictions that would displace it. At its "pinnacle" (e.g., in the works of the great Victorians) the nineteenth-century novel was a Judaized one in that it dealt "with a society of will and commandment." Ozick's call for a Jewish literature that evokes the values of the preceding century rather than those of her own reflects anxiety about the survival of Jewish culture. Unless it is sharply focused on Jewish concerns grounded in traditional religious values, that literature—and the culture it nominally represents—will vanish. Those Jews who call themselves "universalists" serve Gentile culture, not their own. In Shylock's pathetic if eloquent formulation of the Jew as part of Mankind, Shakespeare reduces him to the sum of his common human attributes while implicitly denying him a unique cultural identity. The climactic conversion of Shylock to Christianity completes *The Merchant of Venice*'s cultural invalidation of the Jew. It is some such "conversion" and the consequent "obliteration of our progeny" that Ozick fears in Jewish professions of universalism. And it is no coincidence that she devotes an entire volume (*Bloodshed and Three Novellas*) to fictions in which self-proclaimed Jewish universalists figure prominently. These invariably inauthentic Jews embody varieties of cultureal submergence that edge toward assimilation—and eventual obliteration.

This fear of obliteration—in one or another of its many aspects—runs like a subtextual current through much of Ozick's fiction. While to a non-Jewish American such fear seems groundless, to a Jew it may be omnipresent, even in America. Few envision an American pogrom, but many, including Ozick, see in acculturation and assimilation its cultural equivalents. Implicit in her call for a centrally Jewish literature is its function of preserving and perpetuating Jewish culture. A parallel strategy is to represent in her stories competing artistic—and, for Ozick, ultimately religious—ideologies as a means of invoking Jewish authenticity. At the center of several stories are Jewish artists whose creative decisions are inseparable from their moral convictions. "Usurpation (Other People's Stories)" tests the limits of Jewish art by forcing its protagonist to choose between literary models. Two writers, Agnon and Tchernikhovsky, represent Hebraism and Hellenism respectively. Although both are Jewish, Agnon hews fast to tradition while Tchernikhovsky strays toward paganism. The first-person female narrator, a story writer whose fascination with paganism recalls Ozick's, must choose between "God or god. The Name of Names or Apollo." She is saved from pagan abomination only by the persistence of Jewish memory. An epilogue in Paradise finds Agnon polishing his Nobel Prize (holiness rewarded), Tchernikhovsky enduring the jibes of Canaanite idols (blasphemy punished). In her 1988 essay "S. Y. Agnon and the First Religion" Ozick confirms the revered dean of Hebrew letters as the old writer of Jerusalem who was never mentioned by name in "Usurpation"—though the inclusion of one of his shorter fables provided an "unmistakable clue"—and who incarnates the Jewish writer in fact as well as in fiction. It is primarily because he is a "safe" writer, one who stands for the "principle of Jerusalem versus the principle of exile, . . . redemption versus illusion" and who refuses to let himself be "swallowed up by the forces of obliteration," that Agnon becomes the ideal model for a "liturgical" literature.[28]

In evoking Jewish identity and its attendant conflicts "Usurpation" is a typical Ozick story. What lends it paradigmatic status is the confluence of Ozick's ground theme with her favorite strategy of representing it: the Jewish identity crisis, dramatized in the Pan versus Moses clash of the sacred and the profane as embodied in the choices of a Jewish female artist. These elements had previously converged in "Virility" (*The Pagan Rabbi and Other Stories*) where, however, they had been muted in the service of Ozick's emerging feminism. Thus Edmund Gate's inauthenticity as an artist traces back to his inauthenticity as a Jew. Jewish and artistic authenticity, apparently inseparable, are embodied in Tante Rivka, whose poems he publishes as his own. Phoniness, at once apparent in Gate's name change from Elia Gatoff, is no less apparent in the critics who laud "his" poems as the "Masculine Principle personified" but condescendingly label Tante Rivka's "thin; feminist art." Although "Virility" suggests that the integrity of Jewish art depends upon its maker's integrity as a Jew—Tante Rivka keeps the faith from which her nephew flees—the story is "in fact a feminist tale, . . . more than that, a tract," according to Ozick. In the fictitious critics who downgrade Tante Rivka's poetry, Ozick lambasts those real critics whose pronouncements reflect little more than sexual bias. A 1971 essay, "Previsions of the Demise of the Dancing Dog," recalls her first encounter with the "Ovarian Theory of Literature." Teaching a writing class, she is struck by how her students' response to Flannery O'Connor's *Wise Blood* changes when its author is identified as a woman. Their unquestioned assumption that inherent differences exist between the writing of men and the writing of women launches Ozick's broadside against all such ideas "of literature-as-physiology." The "gratuitous allusion to the writer's sex and its supposed effects" is ever-present in reviews of books written by women. Invariably the distinction between male and female writers is drawn to the disadvantage of the latter. Ozick's conclusion—"Genius is the property of both sexes and all nations alike"—reflects the understandable fear of a writer who happens to be not only a woman but a Jew that her religion could as easily be held against her as her sex.[29] This plea for a humanism that transcends sexual and national identities is also featured in "Literature and the Politics of Sex: A Dissent," a 1977 essay that is reprinted as a companion piece to "Previsions of the Demise of the Dancing Dog" in *Art and Ardor.* Written against the grain of then-current feminist theory, the 1977 essay deplores what Ozick calls, in an explanatory preface, "the headlong development of self-segregation in the women's movement." Classical feminism has been undermined by a "politics of sex"; as used by the "new" feminists the term "woman writer" is both regressive and reductive.[30] Setting women apart from men, such exclusionary tactics simply recall—and reinforce—male sexist postures typified by the reviewers of "Virility."

Women figure more prominently in *Levitation: Five Fictions* than in any other Ozick volume. Yet despite the presence of a female protagonist in each story, feminism

is overshadowed by the essential issue of Jewish identity.
Nowhere is it suggested that a potential rift exists between
feminist and Jewish identitites. But Judaism is notoriously
sexist, and Ozick could not forever ignore a bias that in
other contexts she deplores. In "The Hole/Birth Cata-
logue" (1972), for example, she attacks the Freudian theory that anatomy is destiny for reducing woman to her
role as childbearer. If she is only a childbearer, then
woman is only a "disgorger of corpses. What is a baby-
machine if not also a corpse-maker?" Freud is guilty of
negating the better part of a woman's life by ignoring
"that insatiable in-between which separates the fresh
birth from the cadaver it turns out to be." For Ozick,
Freud's anatomy is destiny is no more than an echo of his
"assertion of the death instinct," itself evidence of "his
hatred for his inherited faith." Her charge—that Freud
"despised Judaism" because it has "above all no slightest
version of death instinct"—makes of him an avatar of
death opposed to "Judaism's declared life principle."[31] To
portray Freudianism as the antithesis of Judaism, a tactic
repeated in "Freud's Room" (*Levitation: Five Fictions*),
is to ignore certain embarrassing points of correspondence. Indeed, the theory that anatomy is destiny evokes
the traditional Jewish female stereotype no less than the
Freudian one.

It is the deliberate and systematic exclusion of Jewish
women "from the collective endeavor of the Jewish people" that provoked Ozick's strongly feminist address to a
seminar at Bar-Ilan University (Israel) in the summer of
1978. Ironically, the failure to allow Jewish women full
participation—resulting in "the mass loss of half of the
available Jewish minds"—seems conformable to Freud's
disenfranchisement of women. Given the millions of

losses suffered in the Holocaust, it is more urgent than ever that Jewish women be granted the right "to share Jewish history to the hilt" with men. "Notes Toward Finding the Right Question," a 1979 article published in the Jewish feminist journal, *Lilith* (No. 6), expands Ozick's argument. One of the most glaring instances of the second-class status of women under Judaism—the separation of the sexes at prayer—elicits this bitter paradox: "My own synagogue is the only place in the world where I am not considered a Jew." Because they are separated from (though theoretically equal to) men, Jewish women are virtually "children and imbeciles." In its institutionalization of injustice toward women, Judaism seems indistinguishable from Freudianism, although Ozick never draws the comparison. So pressing, however, is the need for Judaism to revise its treatment of women that Ozick urges an eleventh commandment: *"Thou shalt not lessen the humanity of women."*[32] If for "women" she had substituted "anyone," Ozick's new commandment would reflect the same transcendent morality that is incarnated in the rich humanism of her art.

NOTES

1. Eve Ottenberg, "The Rich Visions of Cynthia Ozick," *The New York Times Magazine* (10 Apr. 1983): 62.

2. Ozick, "Washington Square, 1946," *Metaphor and Memory* (New York: Knopf, 1989) 112–19.

3. Ozick, "The Lesson of the Master," *Art and Ardor* (New York: Knopf, 1983) 294.

4. *Art and Ardor* 297.

5. Ottenberg 63.

6. Catherine Rainwater and William J. Scheick, "An Interview with Cynthia Ozick (Summer, 1982)," *Texas Studies in Literature and Language* 25 (Summer 1983) 257.

7. "The Seam of the Snail," *Metaphor and Memory* 109–10.

8. Ottenberg 66.

9. Rainwater and Scheick 258.

10. *Art and Ardor* 157. In a prefatory note to the essay, reprinted as "Toward a New Yiddish," Ozick admits that she is "no longer greatly attached to its conclusions." The theory of an indispensable single language (English) Judaized to fashion a Diaspora literary culture is explicitly recanted.

11. *Art and Ardor* 177.

12. Leo Baeck, "Romantic Religion," *Judaism and Christianity,* trans. Walter Kaufmann (Philadelphia: Jewish Publication Society of America, 1958) 189–90.

13. Baeck 291–92.

14. *Art and Ardor* 169.

15. *Metaphor and Memory* 253.

16. *Art and Ardor* 195.

17. *Art and Ardor* 191.

18. Sidra De Koven Ezrahi, *By Words Alone: The Holocaust in Literature* (Chicago: University of Chicago Press, 1980) 53.

19. *Metaphor and Memory* 238.

20. *Metaphor and Memory* 229.

21. Ezrahi 102.

22. *Art and Ardor* 238–39.

23. *Art and Ardor* 247–48.

24. *Metaphor and Memory* 139.

25. *Art and Ardor* 64, 73.

26. *Art and Ardor* 246.

27. *Art and Ardor* 164, 165.

28. *Metaphor and Memory* 222.

29. *Art and Ardor* 266–68; 278.

30. *Art and Ardor* 262.

31. *Art and Ardor* 255, 256.

32. Louis Harap, "The Religious Art of Cynthia Ozick," *Judaism* 33 (1984) 353–63; see esp. 360, 361.

CHAPTER TWO

Trust

During her twenties and thirties literature was
Ozick's religion, its high priest Henry James. And it was
in thralldom to the autonomy, even to the sanctity, of the
Work of Art and to James as its ideal progenitor that *Trust*
(1966) was born.[1] So haunting was the Master's presence
that as a young woman Ozick "was also the elderly bald-
headed Henry James." Like him she was "a worshiper
of literature," a priest at its altar; "and that altar was
all my life."[2] The "cannibalistically ambitious" *Trust*
frankly appropriates James's characterizations, situations,
themes, even locutions in mirroring his high seriousness.
Among the innumerable instances of Jamesian influence
one of the most obvious is also one of the most revealing:
the verbatim quotation of the opening lines of *The Portrait of a Lady*.[3] For although the twenty-two-year-old female narrator remains nameless throughout *Trust*, she is,
like James's Isabel Archer, the subject of a literary portrait. In its concern with feminine identity, but equally in
its single point of view, its elaboration of motive, and its
intricacies of style and metaphor, *Trust* is a Jamesian
novel.

The Portrait of a Lady is typically Jamesian in its theme of initiation, its mostly upper-class characters, and its juxtaposition of Europe and America. While all of these elements likewise appear in *Trust,* the initiation motif predominates, as it so often does in James. Young (Isabel Archer) or old (Lambert Strether in *The Ambassadors*), male or female, James's protagonists are caught up in the process of self-discovery. The unfolding of this process, which dictates the form of so many of his novels, is no less crucial to *Trust.* For Ozick's narrator, however, self-discovery is both more conscious and more literal than it is for James's initiates. Isabel Archer, for example, does not set out deliberately to find herself; only in the process of living does self-knowledge, largely unsought, come about. *Trust*'s young woman, by contrast, is motivated— and obsessed—solely by the need to solve the riddle of her birth—in short to discover, quite literally, who she is. Consequently *Trust* is shaped as a quest, more in the manner of *The Ambassadors* than of *The Portrait of a Lady,* but again with an important difference. Strether's was a quest that ostensibly had little to do with himself; as in the case of Isabel Archer self-knowledge comes unbidden, an ironic by-product of daily living. For the narrator of *Trust,* living can truly commence only after she learns the secret of her birth. Throughout most of the novel she appears to exist in a state of suspended animation, as if awaiting the conferral of the name so long withheld. Because that name is her father's, the theme of self-discovery takes the form of a quest as old as literature itself, except that in *Trust* the conventional search for the father is undertaken not by a son but by a daughter.

Homer's *Odyssey* is the Western literary paradigm of self-discovery consequent upon discovery of the father. Of course Telemachus knows the identity of his father, though not his whereabouts; Ozick's young woman must find out not merely *where* her father is but *who* he is. And her womanhood, like Telemachus's manhood, can be fully attained only in the presence of the father. Telemachus refuses the surrogate fatherhood proffered by his mother's suitors, following the example of Penelope herself, who refuses their proposals of marriage. But Allegra Vand, far from preserving the memory of her former lover—and the narrator's father—attempts constantly, and successfully, to efface it. Not until her daughter is past twenty-one (college graduation marks the real onset of the narrator's need to matriculate into fuller knowledge) does Allegra reluctantly inform her of her illegitimacy. Unwanted at birth, unwelcome thereafter, the narrator had been denied even her own name by a mother whose "aim was to re-father me" (58). Aided and abetted by her first husband, whose name her daughter bears, and by her second husband, with whom she and her daughter live, Allegra has "virtually obliterated from our lives" the father whose name "I was not permitted even to bear," concludes the narrator (9). Even when she accidentally learns the identity of her biological father, he remains no more than a name with an address to which Allegra sends the money he periodically demands. It is the image of Gustave Nicholas Tilbeck as "mendicant" and "leech" that chiefly informs the narrator's first perception of her father's identity.

As in James, money lies at the root of corruption, potentially tainting its actual and would-be possessors alike. Allegra's immense fortune conditions nearly all action and motivation of *Trust*. Held in a trust—one of the many ironies playing about the novel's title—administered by William, Allegra's first husband, the money serves chiefly

to support a vain and idle life style. William's lawyerly
fidelity that survives their broken marriage is bought; it
stems less from his reputed incorruptibility than from his
devotion to wealth. Enoch Vand, his socialist ideals (i.e.,
trust) betrayed by the unholy Hitler-Stalin pact, marries
Allegra only because "when hope is gone, it is good to be
able to fall back on money" (377). Edward McGovern,
who edits *Bushelbasket*, Allegra's pretentious avant-garde
poetry journal, is, like William and Enoch, "bought and
paid for." A poetaster who panders to Allegra's execrable
literary taste, McGovern calls himself "an instance of private enterprise," a luxury "which only the very rich can
afford" (41). Nick Tilbeck abandoned his lover and baby
daughter in Brighton, buying his train ticket with the
money Allegra gave him for breakfast—a double breach
of trust. Never having cared about their daughter ("the
thing," he calls her just before fleeing Brighton), he con-
tinues to care about Allegra's money as her blackmailer.
As parasitical as are the men in her life, they are hardly
more corrupt than Allegra herself. A professed socialist,
she is above all status conscious, harping continually on
matters of prestige and social position and even their ac-
coutrements—clothes, houses, etc. Allegra uses her fortune to bolster her ego (*Bushelbasket*), to enslave (her
husbands, McGovern), to buy off (Nick, the French po-
lice) rather than for any productive purpose. The ball Allegra gives for her daughter's graduation is a form of self-
advertisement: she chooses the guests, the food and drink,
the music, even her daughter's dress—"a blaze of gold
and silver." In this glittering Paris gown which ostentatiously trumpets Allegra's taste—and cash—the narrator
looks "as though you're dressed up in money" (23). The
narrator herself likens the "chink, chink" of her dress to

"the smothered call of greed" (37), perceiving it as the incarnation of her mother's tainted riches: "There was the sick breath of money all upon us; it rushed out dirtily as from a beggar's foul mouth . . . full of waste, clogged with sores and boils" (36).

As though debilitated by money sickness, the youthful partygoers, including the narrator, seem enervated, prematurely world-weary. In their desultory conversation they unconsciously mimic the snobbishly cutting banter and the corrosively cynical outlook of their elders. Nearly all of the personal relationships in *Trust* are similarly afflicted. Sexual betrayal is the rule rather than the exception: Allegra runs away from William to be with Nick, who soon abandons her and their child. A generation later Stefanie betrays her fiancé, William's son, again with Nick. Still, the young man intends to go through with the wedding despite the narrator's warning that Stefanie will surely continue to deceive him. Following William's example, his son will marry more for social and material than for emotional reasons. Allegra's two passionless marriages are equally calculating. And even Mrs. Purse, whose fertility suggests marital equanimity if not ecstasy, routinely cuckolds her husband with Nick. Although they are Quakers whose wants are professedly simple, the aptly named Purses are as greedy as the others. They are downcast when they realize that Nick has no money and that the lavish gifts promised by their supposedly wealthy benefactor will not be forthcoming. After Nick's death Mrs. Purse, having learned that the narrator is Allegra Vand's daughter, writes to her from Pakistan, reminding her of "the very lovely tradition of generosity your memorable father established toward us" and enclosing a list

of "all the children's clothing sizes, including underwear" (566).

Although Allegra Vand and wealth are synonymous—
even her bodily secretions exude money, according to her
daughter—corruption in *Trust* is confined neither to
her immediate circle nor to her social class. Rather, the
rotting neo-Jamesian world of Gentile high society spotlighted in *Trust* is symptomatic of the world at large. The
stench of universal corruption, so faint in the works
of James but so powerful in *Trust,* invokes the chamber of
horrors that constitutes the greater part of twentieth-
century history. Horrified at the outbreak of World War I,
James feared but could envision only dimly the death of
European civilization as he had known it. Ozick, writing
after World War II, reconstitutes James's favorite interna-
tional theme not to revivify a ravaged civilization but to
examine it postmortem. James invariably sent his Americans to Europe to imbibe the air of a culture older and
more complexly imbricated than their own. A rite of passage tantamount to moral initiation, experiencing Europe
is the indispensable prerequisite for living fully. The
heightened sensitivity and sophistication of James's American initiates inevitably leaves them wiser though not necessarily happier. Trapped in a loveless marriage, the
thoroughly Europeanized Isabel Archer is undeniably
wiser yet infinitely sadder at the end of *The Portrait of a
Lady* than she was at the beginning. Allegra Vand, whose
prewar European experience consisted chiefly of shallow
politics and sordid romance—her interlude with Nick at
Brighton was the highlight of her travels and of her life—
wastes little time before returning to Europe once the war
has ended. In Jamesian fashion she equates Europe with

civilization: ''and she promised from this fountain of the world (she called it life, she called it Europe) all spectacle, dominion, energy, and honor,'' recalls the narrator a dozen years later (78). The Europe of Allegra's desires— ''secret and brilliant incarnations of her illusions'' (78)— is a banal redaction of the Europe of Henry James. Reducing Europe to a figment of Allegra's shallow imaginings exposes her cultural pretensions. Yet the spires, minarets, icons, and moats she wishes her daughter to see are most likely the very ones James might have pointed out, albeit with profounder insight.

Ozick's crucial point is not that Allegra fails to invoke James's Europe but that his Europe no longer exists. No sooner does she arrive in Europe ''the very year the war ended'' than Allegra begins whining about the poor quality of milk, food, and accommodations. What impresses her most about the shattered Europe of 1945 is its lack of civilized amenities. It is as though World War II had never occurred; or, having occurred, was merely an annoying nuisance, a momentary inconvenience. Narcissistic as always, Allegra is oblivious to or forgetful of even the most recent past. Unaffected by the greatest cataclysm in human history, she seems blissfully unaware of its tragic dimensions and of Europe as anything but a tourist destination: ''And all the while she never smelled death there,'' marvels the narrator more than once. In her moral blindness Allegra resembles a perverted version of one of James's American innocents abroad. While she is not necessarily *the* representative American, she is at least representative of a typical brand of American folly.

More secure than Allegra's linkage with America is Enoch's with Europe. Although born in Chicago he is identified with Europe not only by Allegra but chiefly by

his own attitudes and perceptions. The stench of death
that eludes Allegra nearly overpowers Enoch: "she could
not smell the death camp gas welling from his eyes" (78).
Allegra rightly guesses that Enoch has been "mastered"
by Europe but wrongly—and ironically—persists in asso-
ciating him with the Europe of spires and minarets, in
short with *her* Europe. Yet Enoch is as impervious to the
romance of postcard Europe as Allegra is to the reality of
postwar Europe. As a bureaucrat assigned the macabre
task of accounting for Holocaust victims, he fills ledgers
with the names of the dead. His interminable lists of Jewish victims constitute their only epitaph and a history of
the Holocaust that engulfed them. It falls upon Enoch as
the novel's only Jew belatedly to bear witness to the destruction of his people. Such witnessings, enjoined upon
all Jews, are sanctified acts of Jewish bonding. No more
than a nominal Jew prior to his close encounter with
"those unshrouded tattooed carcasses of his, moving in
freight cars over the gassed and blighted continent" (78),
Enoch becomes an authentic Jew in the hell that is postwar Europe. These first signs of moral growth prefigure
his formal commitment to Judaism at the end of *Trust* and
arise from an obsession with history that is itself Jewish.

Ozick's pairing of Enoch and Allegra defines Jew and
Gentile in terms of their respective attitudes toward history. Holocaust consciousness is made the touchstone of
historical awareness and thus of moral substance in *Trust,*
as it will prove to be in much of Ozick's later work.
Enoch's confrontation with the Holocaust seems particularly wrenching in light of Allegra's all but amnesiac indifference to the facts of history. Even at the age of ten,
well before she could have understood the Holocaust, the
narrator instinctively rejects Allegra's view of Europe in

favor of her stepfather's. Twice the child imagines the map of Europe—first outlined in the vomit she spews over a German tank, later in the stains made by water, wine, urine, and blood which "shone like crenelated scars and entrails" on her hotel mattress [116]. The Europe of her excremental mappings is the Europe of Enoch's death camp gas. "It's not her fault," explains the narrator's governess when Allegra scolds her daughter for the stench of her vomit: "It is the stink of Europe" (64).

At the end of Part Two: Europe, Allegra jubilantly answers Enoch's cable announcing his promotion with one of her own, closing with "NO MORE CORPSES." Historically myopic as ever, she imagines that a change of assignment and locale will suffice to dispel all memory of the Holocaust. Conversing with Enoch a dozen years later, the narrator unknowingly echoes her mother, calling his present job "clean" and adding that "time makes you forget" (191). Her retreat from history allies her with those who would deny or forget the Holocaust against the novel's lone Jew. Enoch's rejoinder—"There are crimes which time chooses to memorialize instead of mitigate" (192)—certifies the uniqueness of the Holocaust and distances him from everyone else in *Trust*. Because he alone possesses the capacity for moral growth (for "trust" in its most profound sense of drawing nearer to God), he threatens to displace the narrator as the novel's central figure. Even after she meets her father, this long-awaited climax of the quest motif that forms the structural spine of *Trust* arguably comes to nothing. Compared with the impact of the Holocaust on Enoch, the meeting with Nick leaves her virtually unchanged. At the end of *Trust* Enoch completes a quest of his own, one that has led him from worldly despair to Jewish belief. The narrator "went to wed-

dings.'' Unable to hold in her memory the meaning of
what she had seen—and viscerally comprehended—at
ten, the narrator, for all her intelligence and critical insight, is no less moribund than her fellow Gentiles. Unable to forget the stench of evil that welled up around
them in 1945, but which the adult narrator dismisses in a
series of clichés about the cleansing effect of time, Enoch
finally escapes the moral swamp in which everyone else is
mired.

The quest for meaning—embodied most obviously in
Enoch's struggles—runs parallel with the narrator's quest
for her father. What meaning the narrator finally discovers
is invested in her father, so that the successful culmination
of her search for Nick results in her allegiance to the values he represents. Before meeting him, she had known
Nick only as her mother's blackmailer and had therefore
assumed that those values were exclusively monetary. His
were apparently the normative values she had grown up
with whose symbol was money and whose avatar was Allegra. The narrator's perception of a father motivated no
less than her mother by greed powerfully reinforced her
negative (i.e., distrustful) world view. From the matrix of
Allegra's circumambient wealth arises a stench which,
like that pervading post-Holocaust Europe, signals corruption. When Nick reveals, however, that his blackmailing
of Allegra was more for sport than profit and that it would
have ended had Allegra simply refused to pay, the narrator sees him as the champion of positive values opposed
to the money-sickness empitomized by her mother. His apparent revulsion from, or at least disregard of, tainted
money outwardly resembles Enoch's reaction to tainted-
Europe. Both men appear, therefore, to be at odds with
key elements of the prevailing social ethos. Even the

climaxes of their respective disenchantments have general affinities. Revolted by material glitz, Nick withdraws to the woods; revolted by moral anomie, Enoch withdraws to Judaism. It is William, the novel's third father figure, who to a far greater degree than Nick or Enoch embodies its cultural negativism. Potentially positive signifiers are nullified in William: money is equated with greed and status-seeking, sex with repression, religion with hypocrisy. Because the cultural crisis permeating *Trust* is ultimately spiritual, it must ultimately be expressed in religious terms.

Spiritual malaise is so normative in *Trust* as to be taken for granted. Allegra—greedy, shallow, amoral—is the locus of negative values that are symbolized by her great wealth. So immense is her fortune that it seems capable of spreading its stain to the entire world. Allegra's money affects lives and determines actions so markedly that even those characters who sense its corrosive power cannot tear themselves from its orbit. Although Nick and Enoch claim to be able to do without money, both maintain relationships with her that center upon her wealth. Cold cash counts more than maternal warmth in Allegra's relationship with her daughter. The narrator's cynical detachment and emotional aridity derive from an upbringing featured by insults and neglect and all but devoid of common affection, not to say love. A momentary spark of love for William's son which goes out nearly as quickly as it flares up is the closest she comes to sensual passion. Love for Nick—felt by Allegra at Brighton and by the narrator at Duneacres—constitutes the only genuine emotion of mother and daughter but not the only similarity between them.

Although the narrator perceives Allegra's shallowness from her own vantage point of superior intelligence, she is hardly more substantial than her mother, who at least possesses the vitality that is so conspicuously lacking in the narrator. The spiritual emptiness they share is spotlighted in their nearly identical responses to Enoch's moral struggles. Mother and daughter alike regard his inability to forget history's greatest crimes—most notably the Holocaust—as merely tiresome. Neither Allegra nor the narrator wishes to be reminded of 1945 Europe. The former sees Enoch's postwar corpse-counting as no more than a distasteful interruption of their presumably single-minded quest for an ambassadorship. The latter is no less impatient with Enoch's attachment to the past and bored by his harping on "the problem of evil in the universe." Allegra's voice—and morality—reverberates in the narrator's counter to Enoch's desire for something that has nothing to do with money: "Doesn't everything have to do with money?" (189). And like Allegra she has no more truck with God than with history. The narrator marvels equally at Enoch's denial of atheism and at his failure to deny her sardonic assertion that he is waiting for the Messiah. Owing perhaps to her intelligence, the narrator often feels closer to her stepfather than to her mother. What her exchange with Enoch ironically reveals, however, is that the distance between them is far greater than that which separates her from Allegra. More than she knows, the narrator speaks for the mother she derides and the money-sick society she despises. Mother and daughter and the social circle the latter disdains but adheres to symptomize Enoch's "whole world that's been dipped in muck" (191). In their godlessness they epitomize the values of the fallen world that Enoch the Jew struggles to transcend.

Secularism is the prevailing "religion" of *Trust* and Judaism its implied moral antithesis. Christianity, represented chiefly by William and his second wife—and defined by their prejudices—is finally indistinguishable from the materialism it serves. Anti-Semitism characterizes William's Christian piety just as contempt for non-WASPs characterizes his wife's. And William's pious devotion to Allegra's trust fund illustrates the God-Mammon equation at the heart of his Calvinism. As morally bankrupt as secularism, Christianity has no more hope of redeeming the world. A Gentile herself, the narrator nonetheless despises Christianity, likening the Holy Ghost to a "new kind of candy bar" (59) and Christ the Saviour to God's "only begotten dung" (279).

If Allegra's secularism and William's Christianity are sterile and Enoch's Judaism essentially private, there remains in *Trust* an alternative "religion" embodied in Nick. Nick's religion is paganism, Nick himself a modern Dionysus. Like his ancient prototype he is associated with sex—his couplings with Allegra, Stefanie, and Mrs. Purse constitute the entire sexual life of *Trust*—and wine—the narrator recognizes her father as "the one who needed wine" (453). Again like Dionysus, Nick is worshiped by women in his role as a pagan fertility god, his rampant sexuality powerfully contrasting with the relative sexlessness of the other male characters. At least in sexual terms he is the only creative force in *Trust,* fathering the narrator and reenacting the moment of her conception with Stefanie. Their intercourse constitutes an epiphany for the narrator—"I felt I had witnessed the very style of my own creation" (531)—that seals her love for her father. Even prior to witnessing their Dionysian revel the narrator likens the piano Nick plays to an attribute of the pagan deity: "Wine ruled it, the divine Bacchus rolled heels and hips over the teeth of its alligator smile, wide as octaves"

(519). That Nick lives by piano-playing—the creation of
music—further expands his role as a Life Force. Part
Greek, looking like a faun, living in a disused museum on
a Crete-like island, Nick is relentlessly associated with the
ancient world and pagan religion. He is one with the figures from Greek mythology who seem also to inhabit his
island: "*I* dreamed up the Parthenon," he boasts to the
narrator shortly after she likens him to Prometheus, the
fire-stealer. Conceiving the Parthenon and giving fire to
man are creative, not to say civilizing, acts. The Greece
of the mind that Nick claims to inhabit is the legendary
cradle of civilization to which the narrator has symbolically returned in search of her father—and herself. She is
rowed over the water to Nick's island by young Purse,
whom she likens to a centaur, albeit a Norse one. Like
Chiron, the boatman of Greek mythology who plies his
oars between the realm of the living and Hades, the realm
of the dead, the boy is the indispensable mediator between
opposing worlds. In the sense that the narrator associates
fecundity with Nick's island, sterility with the mainland
she has left behind, hers is a passage that reverses the
Greek voyage from life to death.

What the narrator finds out about Nick at Duneacres
her mother had discovered long ago at Brighton. Writing
to William on February 2, 1938, shortly after giving birth
to her daughter and being abandoned by her lover, Allegra
equates Nick with the Life Force. "I never felt grace till
Nick," she gushes (340). "Nick's the one who discovered
I'm a Pagan and half the summer he called me an ancient
Greek" (337). Nick is her "guru," their mattress "religious." She associates him with summer flowers, with a
"holy-looking" tree, with Buddhist rites. Like a pagan
fertility god Nick departs with the end of summer, making

off with Allegra's *Enchiridion* (''my flower book''). Allegra imagines him ''spread out on a beach in the sun'' on Sicily, an island no less evocative of the ancient world than Crete, the island identified with Duneacres—and with Nick—by the narrator many years later. In the wake of Nick's flight from Brighton, what was ''happy and gorgeous, . . . all green'' is no more, ''and out the window there's nothing on the tree but an old stuck dart with dirty snow on its tail'' (344). What Nick represents for Allegra is Sacred Beauty, which she opposes successively to William's Presbyterianism and to Enoch's Social Justice. Sacred, rhapsodizes Allegra, is ''anything that's alive, and Beauty is anything that makes you want to *be* alive and alive forever, with a sort of shining feeling'' (337). By ''shining feeling'' Allegra clearly means the sexual fulfillment she can attain only with Nick. The ''grace'' she feels with Nick at Brighton she failed to achieve with William—''I was dry all the time''—during their summer honeymoon on Cape Ann. Water—source of life, nourisher of the many flowers that for Allegra symbolize her one summer of happiness—flows from Nick, who is endlessly identified with the sea. With the loss of Nick, Allegra's link to nature snaps. It is significant that only at Brighton and Duneacres, proximate to the sea and dominated by Nick, does *Trust* remain very long out-of-doors. Sea imagery plays about Nick most intensely at Duneacres, originally the seaside estate of Allegra's millionaire father, who had directed that it become a marine museum after his death. A man who ''liked to think of himself as a mariner,'' he intended the museum to be ''not just an aquarium'' but a ''History of the Origin of Life'' (296). His allusions to Neptune, to sea nymphs, and above all to ''the majesty of wetness'' ally him with Nick as an enemy of ''dryness.'' As founder of Allegra's trust fund and bequeather of the marine museum, the old man "creates" the chief opposing values—and metaphors—of the novel. Significantly, Allegra "despised" the house that teetered so "pointlessly at the water's edge." She inherits her father's money—the source of death; Nick takes over the marine museum—the source of life. Severed from Nick—and from the Life Force he represents—Allegra, who after Brighton "had given up expectation of renewal," marries Enoch to share with him "the empty aftermath of the extraordinary" (395).

By the end of the Duneacres episode the narrator has achieved the knowledge of her father that was the aim of her quest. Yet full knowledge of Nick would seem contingent upon the same apprehension of Sacred Beauty that Allegra achieved through sexual consummation. Barred by her evident virginity—as well as by her relationship to Nick—from direct participation in the rite of love, she nonetheless gains the requisite knowledge indirectly. The indispensable physical proximity to Nick in his fertility god incarnation occurs when the narrator cuts her hand and Nick recalls "what they do in Sicily . . . to stop a virgin's bleeding, obtain the fresh-sucked saliva of the head of the family." She then tastes his saliva mingled with the blood from her finger: "Carelessly and silently he entered my mouth" (474) Analogous to the communion sacrament with its symbolic ingestion of the body and blood of Christ, the episode combines elements of religious and sexual initiation. A few moments before cutting herself the narrator had addressed her father as Nick for the first time. Thus invoked, Nick in turn invokes Thor and Loki, adding that he (Nick) should have been named Zeus. "Or Pan," replies the narrator presciently. Already Zeus and Pan, Nick becomes Christ as well in the narrator's version of communion. Agent of the Life Force, he is at once father, initiator, and saviour. Later, the narrator's vicarious participation in the final epiphany of her father's intercourse with Stefanie is signaled by her repetition of the communion analogy: "I was initiate. I knew it. I knew the taste of complicity. Nick had put it on my tongue" (520). What Nick enacts physically with Stefanie, he has already enacted symbolically with his daughter via her bleeding finger and their mingled saliva. Still, Nick must render himself immanent in the act of procreation to complete his refathering of the narrator, to imbue his daughter with ultimate knowledge, and finally to generate her emotional transcendence: "I loved my father" (526).

Coming from the notoriously skeptical narrator this simple yet unconditional declaration of love ends her quest on a particularly poignant note. Implied in her clearly heartfelt avowal is the conclusion that the world, certified "unredeemable" by Enoch Vand, can in fact be redeemed by Nick Tilbeck's Sacred Beauty. A phenomenon closely allied with nature, Sacred Beauty is perceived by the narrator in the form of an "extraordinary little tree" showering radiance down upon her and re-creating her as "nymph, naiad, sprite, goddess" (424–25). Like the similarly "holy-looking tree" outside the Brighton cottage that Allegra cited to William as an example of Sacred Beauty and that grew sere after Nick's departure, this one is associated not only with Greek but with Buddhist worship. While her mother's experience was doubtless more ecstatic, the narrator's is hardly less intense. More intelligent than Allegra and more given to critical analysis, the narrator expands the religious imagery of their similar epiphanies. Eventually Nick becomes a "male Muse" whose Sacred Beauty is both creative and salvational. His role expands from the sexual to the sacrificial, from his "death" by sexual consummation to his final death by water. In both climaxes there is the promise of rebirth, a promise that the narrator inflates beyond the personal to the universal. To apprehend Sacred Beauty is to grasp the means by which the spiritually dead—the narrator, the world—may live again.

With the culmination of *Trust*'s enfolded and parallel quests—for the father, for the self, ultimately for meaning—a sharper image of the narrator snaps into focus. Viewed retrospectively, and particularly in the light of Nick's identification as male Muse, the narrator's self-consciousness, detachment, prescience—and anonymity—may add up to "Ozick's portrait of the artist as a young woman."[4] Thus viewed, the narrator's longing for "some impermeable lacquer to enamel an endless youth" (3) equates personal fulfillment with the creation of lasting art; and it is "endless youth," a metaphor for artistic immortality, that is finally conferred upon her by Nick in his role of male Muse. The narrator's highly polished style— "every paragraph a poem"—is that of the conscious artist fashioning not a mere chronicle of events but a literary artifact.[5] That this finished work of art turns out to be, among other things, a parable of the artist (herself) is not surprising. "I hope I've written an occasional parable"— a form in which "story and idea are so inextricably fused that they cannot be torn free of each other"—says Ozick, distinguishing between parable and the "low form" of allegory in which "the idea can be stated entirely apart from the story."[6] Already previewed in her MA thesis— "Parable in the Late Novels of Henry James"—was the fascination with a form (parable) and an author (James) whose influence shape her own fiction. *Trust* contains many examples of fraudulent art—the imitation haiku of Edward McMahon, the punning doggerel of Eugenia Karp, especially the rancid prose of Allegra Vand. And the narrator's "mandarin" and "lapidary" style—Ozick's description of her own style in *Trust* must also apply to her first-person narrator's—constitutes an elegant debunking of the bad art it transcends. *Marianna Harlow,* Allegra's novel, is judged unreadable by her daughter: "It had no style, its unhinged dialogue was indistinguishable from my mother's own prattling, and its chief influence seemed to have been *The Bobbsey Twins*" (15). Although its "subjects were passion and death," Enoch regarded *Marianna Harlow* as a piece of comic art which, "in spite of its bad prose," rewards reading as "a prize example of the lampoon" (15). In *Marianna Harlow* Allegra's symbolic sickness, already abundantly evident in matters of morals and money, extends to the realm of art. In his role as male Muse—"cult in himself . . . the cult of art . . . the cult of experience" (325)—Nick again embodies values, this time artistic ones, that are antithetical to Allegra's. *Trust* is similarly antithetical to *Marianna Harlow.* Inspired by Nick's tutelage, the narrator's "novel" treats her mother's subjects—passion and death—with the high seriousness impossible for Allegra to fathom, much less to attain. If Ozick's portrait of a young woman is a portrait of the artist as well, then the narrator has found not only a father and a self but a vocation.

Given the structure of *Trust,* it falls to the portagonist to interpret as well as to enact the quest. As in any first-person narrative the identity of the central consciousness is all-important. Particularly in a novel whose title "was of course ironic and signified distrust in every cranny," according to Ozick, the reliability of the narrator is no less an issue than the story she relates.[7] Aside from her sexual naïveté Ozick's young woman seems relentlessly knowing. While her abrasive assertions of intellectual superiority—only Enoch and Nick can withstand or reciprocate her verbal slings and arrows—may mask the essential insecurity of the emotionally underdeveloped, her various insights gain credence from the evident perspicacity of their expression. The wasteland atmosphere of *Trust* derives primarily from the narrator's cynicism about people and their motives; it is dispelled only when she encounters a person (Nick) in whom she locates redemptive value (Sacred Beauty).

And it is her sexual innocence that may predispose her to love Nick, the incarnation of sexuality. For the narrator, the epiphany of Nick's lovemaking with Stefanie is as religious as it is sexual. Likening her father to ancient fertility gods, she embraces pagan worship as the means of spiritual renewal. In the natural world revered by the Greeks and incarnated in Nick's Sacred Beauty she locates a value system that promises relief from her soul-sickness. Central to her newfound belief is the creative role of sex—as generative but also as corrective to the sterility she assigns to the Judeo-Christian tradition. Since the narrator's spiritual transfiguration is owed to Nick, its validity hinges ultimately on the truth of what she perceives in her father and his actions. And truth in turn rests upon the accuracy of her perceptions. Given the many Jamesian elements in *Trust*, it is not inconceivable that Ozick's young woman, like so many of James's (e.g., Isabel Archer), knows less than she thinks she does—that, in short, knowledge is treated ironically by Ozick as it is so often by James. In *Trust* the indifference of her mother and stepfather, the emptiness of her life, the blight upon her society, most of all her innocence impel the narrator toward Nick. That his allure is essentially sexual makes him all the more attractive to his sexually backward daughter. The erotically charged atmosphere and heated rhetoric attending Nick magnetize a girl eager for the sexual experience he embodies. And the very suddenness of her ''conversion'' casts suspicion on its authenticity.

Once the perceivers and their perceptions are called into question, then the truth about Nick and what he represents must be reexamined. Even at his zenith in the ''Dune-acres'' section of *Trust,* when the narrator's worship reaches fever pitch, Nick remains an ambiguous figure. Stefanie assures him that she is ''stuffed to the gills'' with contraceptives just before the bout of lovemaking that certifies Nick as the Life Force and that inspires the narrator's love. But for an ''avatar of a pagan fertility god'' Nick's generative powers are compromised.[8] The one child he fathered—abandoned along with her mother—he repudiated by twenty-one years of neglect. And while it might be argued that the bestial lovemaking of Nick and Stefanie celebrates the liberating force of unalloyed sex, it might just as easily be argued that it negates whatever emotional involvement separates human from animal sexuality. ''From the beginning,'' recalls the narrator, ''they never kissed'' (531). ''Not wanting anything is what makes one perfectly free,'' Nick informs his daughter. ''There's not a thing in the wide world I want. Or ever wanted'' (468). It is true that his lack of wants spares Nick from material corruption, but it also shields him from commitment. Actually he is as selfish in his own way as Allegra is in hers: it is no coincidence that they both dislike their baby from the moment of its birth. The bottle containing Nick's last words, washed ashore after his drowning, "smelled of wine but did not taste of it" (535). This hint of evanescence typifies Nick's elusiveness: "Whatever you think I am, that's what I'm not," he had boasted to the narrator (510). Refusing a stable identity is tantamount to denying material wants: both are modes of evasion that deliberately foreclose any but the briefest of commitments. In failing even to sign his final note Nick maintains in death the disengagement that shaped his life: "The mind that set the letters down loved no one," admits the narrator (535).

Although his apparent lack of concern in no way diminishes his daughter's love, his death and its aftermath mirror the doubtful authenticity of Nick's life. A "tawdry Muse" whose squalid death evokes neither the sacrificial meaning nor the redemptive promise attendant upon the demise of fertility gods, Nick seems ultimately to represent nothing more profound than himself. He is deified chiefly by a callow young woman whose susceptibility reflects her own sexual backwardness. William's counter to the narrator's view of Nick (the "cult of art . . . of experience") contains more than a grain of truth: "the cult of the cheat" (325). Not awe but irony attends Nick's death: his hair "was dyed blond: his body was covered with vomit" (536). And the flower imagery playing about Nick living is putrified in the vomit enveloping Nick dead: "The skein had clotted into islands of tender putrid greenish flowers, and his falsely bright head was covered" (545). If Europe's corruption was traced in the narrator's vomit, the corruption of Duneacres is traced no less clearly in Nick's. It is significant that Nick is worshiped only by three women—the fatuous Allegra, the brainless Stefanie, and the impressionable narrator. Allegra grieves more for Enoch's lost embassy than for the dead Nick.

And the narrator, having enshrined Nick in her memory, evidences little growth after her father's death. At the end of *Trust* she again attends weddings that recall the "shimmer of mass marriages," the coalescence of "all the weddings of the world" (3) with which the novel began. She remains as "deprived of that seductive bridegroom" as ever, no more emotionally fulfilled than she was at the moment when her college commencement first signaled the onset of maturity.

It is Enoch Vand who alone demonstrates the capacity for growth that in quest novels is traditionally assigned to the protagonist. Allegra's social ambitions, Nick's moral irresponsibility, the narrator's icy detachment—all are strategies of accommodation to a blighted status quo. Only Enoch strives to fathom the universal woe, the terrible mechanism that turns "that lovely marvel, man . . . into a carbon speck." Of course it was in the Holocaust incinerator that man became ash, that the "metaphysics of the immortality of the race" yielded to the conviction that "grit . . . alone endures" (373). Notably missing in the others is Enoch's wrenching struggle for belief. In the last pages of *Trust* the outcome of *his* quest for a faith to live by undermines and trivializes that of the narrator. The climactic placement and ultimate meaning of Enoch's return to Jewishness transforms what had appeared to be a muted counterpoint to the central quest motif into its transcendent realization. All along Enoch had embodied Hebraic principles in conflict with the Hellenic principles incarnated in Nick. "Pan Versus Moses"—"a Jewish sort of essay"—is the title of Enoch's projected study of how Moses makes the Israelites destroy pagan shrines, of "how Moses hates Nature" (557). That Ozick first invokes Hebraism triumphant, then devotes an entire

chapter to Enoch's "maxims," and finally documents his
re-Judaization, all in *Trust*'s last eleven pages, effectively
demolishes the pagan edifice—crumbling in any event—
that the narrator saw in Duneacres. In rejecting paganism
for Judaism, Nick's way for Enoch's, Ozick recapitulates
her own spiritual development. "Greeks and Jews," the
title of her unpublished volume of poetry, reflects the
same tension between pagan and Jewish belief explicit in
Enoch's "Pan Versus Moses" essay. By the time she had
completed *Trust*, Ozick the aesthete had turned into Ozick
the Jew. "Until very recently," she confesses in 1970,
"my whole life was given over to the religion of Art."[9]
Trust, begun "for the Gentiles" but "finished" for the
Jews, therefore records in its ending the moral evolution
of its author. "I began as an American novelist and ended
as a Jewish novelist. I Judaized myself as I wrote it."[10]

Enoch's Judaization—though not its centrality in re-
solving the moral crisis of *Trust*—is adumbrated early in
the novel. In his moral and intellectual proximity to the
Holocaust, in his reverence for the word and his postwar
role as witness/historian, in his "waiting for the Messiah," Enoch reflects an essential Jewishness that wants
only formal articulation. Allegra, believing his "old job"
of counting concentration camp victims had *"ruined"*
him, admonishing him for "talking like a Jew," maintain-
ing along with her daughter that the "concentration
camps are all over!" ironically calls attention to the moral
distance separating Enoch from all the other characters in
Trust (197–98). While it is true that his cynical marriage
to Allegra and his abject surrender to her social aspira-
tions reflect the postwar despair of a man who, sickened
by Holocaust atrocities, judges the world "unredeemable," it is equally true that even this spiritual nadir is

recognizably Jewish. The massive destruction of European
Jewry forced those Jews who remained alive into a stark
confrontation with the precepts that had formerly sustained them. Many, like Enoch, yielded up their traditional Jewish belief ''that whatever you come upon that
seems unredeemed exists for the sake of permitting you
the sacred opportunity to redeem it'' (398) along with its
corollary: the belief in the special relationship between
God and His chosen people. Yet this wholly understandable crisis of confidence was itself often the starting point
for a spiritual inventory that might, as in Enoch's case,
inspire religious renewal. In other words, Enoch's loss of
faith no less than its recovery evokes the post-Holocaust
Jewish experience.

Long before he becomes an orthodox Jew, Enoch the
''apostate'' is linked by the narrator not only to the Holocaust but to events equally important in the formation of
Jewish identity: ''I saw him: he had been formed at Creation, he had been witness at Sinai'' (201). This inherent
Jewishness surfaces, for example, in his politics. A casu-
alty of the Hitler-Stalin pact, Enoch's once passionate socialism typifies the Jewish prewar quest for social justice.
Even his postwar conservative turn—his Republican party
membership may, however, more accurately reflect Allegra's ambitions than his own convictions—conforms to a
familiar Jewish pattern, as does his ultimate decision for
spiritual renewal. Beneath an apparent inconsistency of
actions lies a profound consistency of aims: to make sense
of a seemingly senseless world and by so doing to formu-
late a morality of existence. Socialism, Republicanism,
marriage to Allegra, angling for an embassy—the various
adjustments of a disaffected Jew unable or unwilling to
commit himself to Judaism—reflect Enoch's belief, a leg-

acy of Jewish suffering culminating in the Holocaust, that
the world is innately evil. Like many Jews, Enoch takes
the concentration camp and its machinery of extermination as a metaphor for the modern world. During the Holocaust God "turned his back on being God" (190); after
the Holocaust he could only be "the God of an unredeemed monstrosity" (397). For Enoch the momentary
solace of politics or marriage can provide no more than a
refuge from his true vocation: "I thought I would be a
monk" (397). Judaism having no monks, he jokingly attributes the failure of belief that actually stems from "absolute rejection, . . . absolute revulsion, absolute
cynicism" to a systemic flaw in his religion (396).

Yet he never forswears Jewishness. Always he knows
wherein to place his trust, should it ever prove possible
for him to do so. The comic scenario of the lost embassy
creates the excuse—in reality the long-awaited signal—
for spiritual rebirth. What Allegra takes for defeat—and
death—Enoch interprets as freedom—and life. By an accident that smacks of God's design Enoch is granted the
opportunity to fulfill his pledge: "Let God be the kind of
God who would allow the sort of world in which it is
possible to lead a virtuous life, and I would repay him by
dedicating my days and every so often my nights to constant praise of his holy name" (397). When Enoch embraces Jewish orthodoxy, he has been given little evidence
that the "unredeemable" world has been miraculously
transfigured. God has not created the world anew; rather
He has liberated Enoch from the snare of worldliness.
Freed by God's grace and by his own expanded moral vision, Enoch—like the many penitents in Isaac Bashevis
Singer's fiction—forsakes the profane for the sacred, nature for covenant, Pan for Moses. In rejecting worldliness

he does not propose to reject the world. But "man must abandon what has enslaved him" or "he has acquiesced to evil" (374–75). Christ is "one of Enoch's great villains" because he rendered unto Caesar "Caesar's evil unmodified"; because he removed "the Kingdom of Heaven to heaven"; and because he misrepresented God, "a principle which it is blasphemy to visualize." In summarizing Enoch's views—"against Christ; against Romance; against Imagination"—the narrator previews those Ozick later expresses in nearly identical language (e.g., in the preface to *Bloodshed and Three Novellas*). It is a distorted religious imagination that sees Pan in Nick, God in Christ. Opposed to Jewish monotheism, such blasphemous incarnations of God evoke for Enoch—and for Ozick—the "apparatus of Romance." Not in Romance, nor in the Party that attracted Enoch or the High Art that tempted Ozick, does the Ideal reside. That the Ideal which alone may redeem human evil is to be found exclusively in "the personal and individual act of a man covenanting on his own behalf" (375) is the discovery of both Enoch and Ozick—and the transcendent theme of *Trust*.

NOTES

1. Ozick, *Art and Ardor* (New York: Knopf, 1983) 157. "When at last I wrote a huge novel I meant it to be a Work of Art," says Ozick of *Trust*. Her capital letters and her immediately preceding confession—"In my twenties I lived the life of the elderly Henry James"—testify to her concept of the high seriousness of literature and the monastic dedication demanded of its acolytes.

2. *Art and Ardor* 294.

3. Ozick, *Trust* (New York: New American Library, 1966) 451. Pages references in parentheses are to this edition.

4. Victor Strandberg, "The Art of Cynthia Ozick," *Texas Studies in Literature and Language* 25 (Summer 1983) 291.

5. Ozick, preface to *Bloodshed and Three Novellas* (New York: Knopf, 1976) 4. "That novel [*Trust*], the product of my education both as student and autodidact in the forties and fifties, cared about High Art and its issues; it was conceived in a style both 'mandarin' and 'lapidary,' every paragraph a poem."

6. Catherine Rainwater and William J. Scheick, "An Interview with Cynthia Ozick (Summer 1982)," *Texas Studies in Literature and Language* 25 (Summer 1983) 262–63.

7. Strandberg 291.

8. Strandberg 280. The interpretation of Nick is overwhelmingly favorable: "Tilbeck's role as avatar of a pagan fertility god enables him to lift his daughter from the mire of Christian/Mosaic 'uncleanness' that would otherwise enclose her identity as 'bastard' or 'illegitimate' issue."

9. *Art and Ardor* 157.

10. Diane Cole, "Cynthia Ozick," *Twentieth-Century American-Jewish Fiction Writers*, ed. Daniel Walden; vol. 28, *Dictionary of Literary Biography* (Detroit: Gale Research, 1984) 215.

CHAPTER THREE

The Pagan Rabbi and Other Stories

At the end of *Trust,* Enoch Vand (né Adam Gruenhorn) begins the arduous process of turning himself back into a Jew. Under the tutelage of a bearded Holocaust survivor whose concentration camp number, tattooed on his forearm, "was daily covered by phylacteries" (567), Vand studies Hebrew. After devoting three years to reading the entire Bible in Hebrew, he finishes *The Ethics of the Fathers* in two months and is ready to take up the Talmud when *Trust* ends. Jewish authenticity—embodied in his teacher's beard, tattoo, and prayer implements no less than in Hebrew and holy texts—is Vand's goal as it will eventually prove to be Ozick's dominant theme. Coming as it does at the end of a novel begun "for the Gentiles" and finished for the Jews, Vand's self-willed conversion parallels Ozick's own deliberate transition from an American novelist to a Jewish storyteller. By 1970 she had jettisoned the "religion of Art" for "liturgical" writing in which aesthetic niceties would take a back seat to Jewish values. Fueled by "moral imagination," Ozick's fiction would henceforth resonate with a

58

"communal voice: the echo of the voice of the Lord of History."[1]

While not all of the writing in *The Pagan Rabbi and Other Stories* (1971) satisfies the demands of the "liturgical," Ozick signals her commitment to a predominantly religious point of view by making "The Pagan Rabbi"— the volume's most deeply Jewish fiction—its title story. Anticipating the theme of "The Pagan Rabbi" (1966), however, is "The Butterfly and the Traffic Light" (1961), the earliest story in the collection. Published in the midst of her prodigious labors (1957–63) on *Trust,* this brief sketch rehearses Ozick's fuller treatment of Jewish identity in "The Pagan Rabbi" even as it testifies to the long gestation of what is to become her dominant theme. The contrast between Jerusalem, where street names "have been forgotten a thousand years," and American cities, where only street names impose centrality upon formlessness, functions as a prelude to the slight main action of "The Butterfly and the Traffic Light." That action consists merely of Fishbein and Isabel conversing in the course of a walk down Big Road, the blandly named main thoroughfare of an unnamed city that could be Anywhere, USA. Fishbein, a Jewish intellectual, is ill at ease in the society of this midwestern university town. To this "imitation of a city" he opposes the world's ancient and fabled capitals which he vociferously prefers. And because Jerusalem, quintessentially Jewish, is invoked as the epitome of the city hallowed by history and the antithesis of the anonymous American city, invariably Gentile, Fishbein's advocacy seems tantamount to Jewish affiliation.

The first of the story's two central metaphors reinforces Fishbein's apparent Jewishness: although he is attracted to the strolling girls in their summer dresses who sprout "like tapestry blossoms" on the sidewalks, he likens them to the transitory butterfly whose fate is waste. Beautiful but ephemeral, the butterfly compares unfavorably to the uglier caterpillar in which "we can regard the better joy of becoming."[2] If butterfly and caterpillar alike are metaphors for art—the former signifying the finished work, the latter the creative process—then Fishbein may simply be expressing an aesthetic preference. But if the "better joy" relates to the liturgical; if, in other words, butterfly and caterpillar stand respectively for profane and sacred art, then Fishbein's preference is at least as religious (i.e., Jewish) as it is aesthetic. The second metaphor of the title is less ambiguous, and it is in Fishbein's reaction to Isabel's likening of a redundant traffic light over Big Road to "some kind of religious icon with a red and a green eye" (214) that his essential antipathy to Judaism is revealed. Stressing their sameness, Fishbein denies that traffic lights could ever be icons, since "What kind of religion would it be which had only one version of its deity?" (214). "An advanced religion. I mean a monotheistic one," replies Isabel, symbolically invoking Judaism as the religion which in its transcendent achievement gave birth to monotheism. Fishbein denies the intrinsic superiority of monotheism, arguing for the accommodation of "Zeus *and* God under one roof" (215). Although he is himself a Jew, if only a nominal one, Fishbein maintains that "only the Jews and their imitators . . . insist on a rigid unitarian God" (215). Attracted to the many gods of classical antiquity, he denies the essence of Judaism and his own Jewishness (not "we Jews" but "the Jews" believe inflexibly in one God). In Fishbein, Ozick invokes for the first time the apostate Jew, a recurring figure in her later fiction. "The

Butterfly and the Traffic Light'' thus foreshadows more exhaustive treatments of her overarching theme—Jewish identity—and hints at her primary strategy—the Hellenism/Hebraism dichotomy—for expressing it.

The title of ''The Pagan Rabbi'' rehearses the clash of opposing theologies that the story dramatizes. Just as ''pagan'' is incompatible with ''rabbi,'' so passion for nature is incompatible with Judaism. That Ozick's rabbi eddies perilously between Jewish and pagan belief is betrayed by his name—an unlikely mingling of the biblical (Isaac) with the pantheistic (Kornfeld). Nor are the oppositions of ''The Pagan Rabbi'' confined to title or a name: the entire story is grounded in a series of similar contrasts between what is Jewish and what is not. Even before the story opens, its epigraph—about breaking off studying to remark upon the beauty of nature—previews its central dichotomy. Drawn from *The Ethics of the Fathers* (one of the Hebrew texts read by Enoch Vand apropos of reasserting his Jewishness at the end of *Trust*) the epigraph sounds a cautionary note in judging its erring rabbi: ''Scripture regards such a one as having hurt his own being'' (3). The fathers of Isaac and the narrator, themselves rabbis, echo the epigraph in their belief that philosophy is a ''corridor'' to the ultimate ''abomination''—idolatry. Implicit in the fathers' warnings is their certainty that moral peril lurks just beyond the Jewish pale. Both Isaac's suicide and the narrator's apostasy result from the philosophical waywardness that led them respectively to pantheism and atheism. Jewish literature abounds with stories of sons who stray from the ethics of the fathers, invariably with disastrous results. The Faustian strain—potentially heroic for Gentiles—that manifests itself most often in a fever to enlarge or transgress the boundaries of the traditional—is anathema to pious Jews. A classic account of the wages of intellectual hubris is given by Isaac Bashevis Singer in his massive novel *The Family Moskat*. In the aimless and futile career of Asa Heshel Bannet, another rabbi's son, Singer traces the many dislocations that eventually come to symbolize the breakdown of traditional values and the breakup of the Jewish family and community, and even to foreshadow the ultimate chaos of the Holocaust. While "The Pagan Rabbi" ostensibly focuses on the fate of a single erring Jew, it reverberates with the same fear for the fate of all Jews, the narrator included.

Isaac Kornfeld's suicide—a radical example of the self-destructive action of Rabbi Jacob's nature worshiper in the epigraph—is announced in the first sentence of "The Pagan Rabbi." Thereafter "The Pagan Rabbi" evolves into a kind of detective story: the narrator, in quest of understanding, goes first to Trilham's Inlet, the site of the suicide; then to Sheindel, Isaac's widow. To learn why Isaac hanged himself is to learn what sort of man Isaac had become, and thereby to unlearn what had formerly passed for the truth about Isaac. Not surprisingly, the process of discovery leads the narrator into a series of reappraisals of his friend's life that reveal hitherto unsuspected affinities with his own. Thus his dropping out of the seminary, marrying and divorcing a Gentile, alienating his father—all conventional indices of apostasy—are writ large in Isaac's definitive transgression. As is often the case in Jewish literature, erudition begets doubt, doubt apostasy. From sacred texts Isaac branches out to profane literature, eventually to embrace the Spinozist heresy: that reality is one substance with an infinite number of attributes of which only thought and extension may be apprehended by

The Pagan Rabbi and Other Stories

human intelligence. Redolent of polytheism and therefore anathema to pious Jews, the philosophy of Spinoza is conventionally invoked in opposition to traditional belief. That Asa Heshel Bannet goes nowhere without his copy of Spinoza's *Ethics* immediately signals his flawed Jewishness in *The Family Moskat*. And Isaac Bashevis Singer himself struggled for years to overcome his early attraction to Spinoza, who more than any other secular writer represents the dangers of forbidden knowledge.

For Isaac Kornfeld such knowledge took the form of a deepening fixation with nature. Sheindel's conviction that if her husband "had been faithful to his books he would have lived" (12) seems at first paradoxical in light of the rabbi's scholarly reputation. What Sheindel means, however, is not that Isaac stopped reading but that he no longer read *his* (i.e., holy) books. Instead he began compulsively to devour books on agronomy, horticulture—in short, on anything pertaining to nature. His insistence on picnics, his joining a hiking club, his writing of fairy tales full of "sprites, nymphs, gods"—all manifestations of a sudden passion for nature and the outdoors—prefigure the astonishing last words of his notebook: "Great Pan lives" (17). It is this apparently deep immersion in paganism that lends credence to Sheindel's no less astonishing remark that Isaac "was never a Jew" (13). An offshoot of the Spinozist heresy of perceiving the one in the many, pantheism nullifies the Second Commandment, the keystone of Judaism. In the transformed Rabbi Kornfeld is the antithesis of one of the classic figures of Jewish literature—the pale and pious scholar buried in holy texts, all but entombed in his study. In the light of traditional Jewish values the narrator's point that "fathers like ours don't know how to love. They live too much indoors" (5) becomes a devastatingly ironic commentary not on the fancied inadequacies of the fathers but on the real shortcomings of the sons. It is the enclosed world of the study rather than the boundless world of external nature that is the proper province for the believing Jew.

Jewish orthodoxy is expressed in Isaac's vision of a bearded old man, bent under the burden of a bag stuffed with holy books, who identifies himself as Isaac's soul. No longer part of Isaac, and therefore lost to him, the old Jew trudges along reading the Law, prayer shawl drooping "on his studious back," oblivious to the beauty of surrounding nature. Significantly, this aged—and age-old—representative of Jewishness appears to Isaac only after the latter has committed the irrevocable sin of coupling with a dryad. In its total abandonment to pagan values this aberrant sexual union triggers the loss of soul signified by the old man's sudden appearance. Whether the dryad's simultaneous disappearance symbolizes the defeat of Pan by Moses—of the ephemerally pagan by the everlastingly Jewish—or merely Isaac's belated awareness that like Dr. Faustus he has lost his soul and gained nothing in return, it seals Isaac's fate. His suicide, the predictable result of this double loss—of pagan nature and Jewish law—is immediately provoked by the old man's reminder of what Isaac should never have forgotten: the Law sounds "more beautiful than the crickets," smells "more radiant than the moss," and tastes better than "clear water" (36). Powerfully expressive of Isaac's failure to resolve theological conflict is his method of suicide: he hangs himself with his soul's prayer shawl from his beloved's body, the young oak tree. Isaac's last words summon the dryad: "For pity of me, come, come." Although her reappearance most probably would have neither alleviated his despair nor averted his suicide, her absence suggests the final inefficacy of the paganism to which Isaac succumbed. Accepting the Jewish Book Council Award for *The Pagan Rabbi and Other Stores* in 1972, Ozick underlined the lesson of her title story: "What is holy is not natural and what is natural is not holy. The God of the Jews must not be conceived of as belonging to nature."

Isaac's long letter, an explanatory confession that fleshes out the implications of his notebook, traces his growing absorption with nature and his foredoomed attempt to reconcile nature worship with Judaism. So desperate was his desire to bridge the gap between pagan and Jewish belief that he imagined a Moses who withheld the "truths" about "the world of Nature" not out of "ignorance" but only because his followers "would have scoffed" (22). Isaac's revisionist estimate of Moses demonstrates the absurd lengths to which he will go to reconcile pagan multiplicity with Jewish monotheism. His many arguments in favor of freeing man's "indwelling" soul from the prison of his body have little to do with Judaism but everything to do with paganism and serve only to foreshadow his total immersion in nature. Not the least of Isaac's transgressions is this desire to detach soul from body, thereby denying the traditional Jewish view that both are inseparable components of a single being and together determine human essence. Again the Hebraic/Hellenic dichotomy is dramatized by an opposition, this time between Sheindel and the dryad with whom Isaac falls in love. Ozick's rabbi forsakes his quintessentially Jewish wife—a Holocaust survivor born in a concentration camp—for a pagan dryad whose girlish form emanates from a tree. An early instance of Ozick's literary strategy of leavening reality with the supernatural as a means of thematic definition, Isaac's coupling with a tree nymph symbolizes his attachment to nature and his detachment from Judaism. Like many fictional Jews who gravitate toward the perceived glitter of external society, he distorts his essential nature by opting for paganism. And Isaac proves no exception to the rule that such Jews self-destruct: "You have spoiled yourself, spoiled yourself with confusions," explains the dryad (33). Soon thereafter, spoliation finds its most radical expression in suicide.

Seeking in nature to free his imagined soul, Isaac finds in the old man the true (i.e., Jewish) soul he unwittingly abandoned. With the materialization of the old man, signifying the soul detached from and thereby lost to the body, comes the end of Isaac's quest and his symbolic death. Since a soulless man is a contradiction in terms—especially in the moral terms that Judaism espouses and the rabbi cannot escape—Isaac's physical death is but the inevitable culmination of a process that began when he first sighted the old man. Her husband's tragic end elicits only contempt from Sheindel, the embodiment of Jewish orthodoxy. No pity is due the suicide, for "he who takes his own life does an abomination" (37). More sympathetic than Sheindel toward Isaac, the narrator nonetheless flushes down the toilet three green house plants which will eventually make their way to Trilham's Inlet, there to decay "amid the civic excrement." A modest and nearly comic gesture, his disposal of greenery evidences an aversion to nature concomitant with a commitment to Judaism.

Still, the narrator's final position is ambiguous. An atheist whose apostasy at least hastened his father's death if it did not kill him outright, the narrator seems to be turning, however slowly and tentatively, back to Judaism.

The Pagan Rabbi and Other Stories

In his love for Sheindel, and in the section of his bookstore devoted to theological works ("chiefly in Hebrew and Aramaic") which he wishes his father could have seen, no less than in his ridding himself of plants, there are hints of Jewish affiliation. At the time of Isaac's suicide the narrator seems to have come to a crossroads in his own life. Just as Isaac's straying from Sheindel represents a step away from Judaism, the narrator's attraction to Sheindel represents a step toward Judaism. Wanting from Sheindel an explanation of Isaac's suicide, the narrator admits that he wants Sheindel herself. Like many quest stories, "The Pagan Rabbi" counterpoints the search for another with the search for the self. A potential convergence of identities typical in such stories results from the essential Jewishness shared by Isaac and the narrator. In Isaac's case the epiphany of loss triggered by the old man's appearance has a finality about it—it is, after all, a human soul that has been irretrievably lost—that leads him inexorably to suicide. The narrator's ultimate destiny is far less conclusive. Drawn to Sheindel—and symbolically, to Judaism—he nonetheless walks out on her in the end. Shaken by her pitilessness, the narrator intuits the requirements of their prospective union. Too weak in his flickering faith to share with her the uncompromising Jewishness for which she stands, he beats a hasty retreat. In his flight from her—and perhaps from himself—the narrator proves finally unable to shoulder the full burden of Jewish identity.

The tension announced by the title of "The Pagan Rabbi" and engendered by Isaac's oscillation between Pan and Moses is virtually nonexistent in an otherwise similar story—"The Dock-Witch." Again a protagonist is fatally attracted to a pagan nymph, and again the story's structure

mirrors the stages of his obsession. Missing the key ingre-
dient of Jewishness, however, "The Dock-Witch" treats
sexual obsession not as a means but as an end. What is
central to "The Pagan Rabbi" is not Isaac's sexual liaison
with the dryad but its religious implications. Sexual union
with what is essentially a tree becomes the final abomination that seals his abandonment of Judaism and his confir-
mation in pantheism. No such opposition between the
sacred and the profane exists in the exclusively secular en-
vironment of "The Dock-Witch." A Gentile and a corporate lawyer rather than a Jew and a rabbi, George, the
first-person narrator of "The Dock-Witch," possesses neither the religion nor the vocation that confers tragic meaning on Isaac's fate. Moreover, the wages of sin (itself
problematical in the diminished world of "The Dock-
Witch") are not the loss of soul and life suffered by an
apostate rabbi but only the loss of job and confidence suffered by a callow adventurer. Lacking the high stakes of a
salvation or damnation scenario, "The Dock-Witch" becomes a seriocomic episode—a disruptive but by no
means fatal encounter with a bewitching older woman—in
the life of an ordinary young man. Undine, the *femme fatale* of "The Dock-Witch," is no less representative of the
natural world than is the equally supernatural dryad in
"The Pagan Rabbi." Since she is a water-sprite instead of
a tree nymph, Undine's powers of enchantment replicate
the siren song of the sea. No less than Isaac's dryad, however, Undine symbolizes primeval nature: like the obviously Hellenic dryad, the Greek-and-Phoenician-singing
Undine incarnates the pagan world.

To an even greater degree than "The Pagan Rabbi,"
"The Dock-Witch" is a story of metamorphosis. George
is a transplanted Midwesterner, an Ohio landlubber lately

come to New York and proximity to the sea. The "only one of my family to turn Easterner" (131), he has forsaken the "clear open purity of the land" (132). Having exchanged a provincial hamlet first for Yale Law School, then for a Manhattan high-rise, George has all the lineaments of the archetypal young man on the make. Yet neither his upwardly mobile job with a prestigious law firm nor his extracurricular life—circumscribed by the requirements of his job and consisting chiefly of seeing traveling Ohioans off at the docks—fits the glamorous stereotype of New York city life. Beneath George's outward assurance about his present life and future prospects Ozick counterpoints a subtle subtext of doubt that his inflated salary is worth its as yet unreckoned price. In any event, George compensates for his constricted life of "grinding away" at the office with similar young men "from landlocked interior towns" with increasingly ecstatic dreams of ships named after queens and docked nearby.

Because George's firm works "for a group of immense, mystically integrated shipping companies," he and the other young lawyers feel the sea in their papers and salt their banter with nautical imagery. More and more George falls under the spell of the sea, its magic heightened and symbolized by reading Conrad "far into the night and every night, novel after novel" (134). In the first several pages of "The Dock-Witch" the sea embodies for George the freedom and romance so conspicuously lacking in his everyday life. After he meets Sylvia (Undine), however, the lure of the sea grows irresistible, its symbolism ambiguous if not sinister. At first George sacrifices lunch hours "to her queer company," falling behind at work. Temporarily breaking the spell cast by this "triviality, a druggist's wife, a crank who hung around the docks"

(146), he sleeps only fitfully, gives up reading at night, finally roams the riverside. But the "river was not enough," its "stinking water" no fit surrogate for the sea. The river's garbage recalls filthy Trilham's Inlet, the scene of Isaac's suicide, but with a key difference: in "The Pagan Rabbi" the water's stench represents corrupt nature; in "The Dock-Witch" it represents nature corrupted. In a Jewish context nature—that which the Law is not—is by definition corrupt; in a secular context a piece of nature has merely been polluted. Isaac ends amidst corrupt nature; George, revolted by nature corrupted, yearns more compulsively than ever for the purer nature of the sea. That only the open sea will do occurs to George as he contemplates the "tame water"—"not savage enough . . . not salt enough" (147)—from the deck of the Staten Island Ferry. At church the text depicting God's casting Jonah into the depths of the sea prompts George to vomit. A biblical reference in a conspicuously secular story, the Jonah episode sounds a cautionary note about the sea's dangers. But although George's "atavistic" attendance at church seems to assert the pull of home and family—of all that is associated with land—the pull of the sea proves stronger. It is his surrender to the sea—and to the forces of nature—that is dramatized in his affair with Undine.

In her several metamorphoses—from Sylvia, matronly druggist's wife; to Undine, sexually insatiable femme fatale; to pagan sea nymph; finally to massive figurehead on the prow of an ancient Viking ship—the dock-witch completes her transition from ordinary woman to ageless personification. Heralded by a host of minor details—dislike of air-conditioning and cosmetics ("nothing touches *my* face . . . only water"); superhuman sexual appetite and strength (an "easy slap" breaks off the knob of a bed-post); singing in forgotten languages to the accompani-ment of an ancient lyre—her changes record George's deepening immersion in nature. Yet despite the evi-dence—his wrecked career and apartment—of Undine's malign influence and against the advice of Uncle Al—"go deep inside a country, away from the shore line, if you want decency" (168)—George races to the docks. There he joins Undine's druggist husband in bewailing their common loss. Fixed on the ship's prow, the wooden Undine mutely testifies to the futility of George, of the druggist, of all men who seek in nature more than nature can offer. Imagining transcendence, they achieve only frustration. That George partly comprehends this lesson is evident in his response to the druggist's "I wish you luck with things when you find out." "Find out what?" asks George "in the voice of a victim" (171). Aware of his victimization—abandoned by Undine, alienated from the "fields of home"—George nevertheless remains unaware that immersion in nature is a dead end. Far shallower than Isaac Kornfeld, George can envision no viable alternative to the patent folly of pantheism. And the symbolic oppo-sition of fields of home and the docks of Mahhattan lacks both the moral issue and the mortal consequences of the opposition of the Law and levity in "The Pagan Rabbi." The failure of the natural world leaves Isaac dead, George merely puzzled.

That two such radically dissimilar characters as Isaac and George fall under the spell of pagan deities suggests an underlying consonance of motives. Diminished exem-plars of the Faustian spirit that equates fulfillment with transcendence, they seek in pantheism a heightened mode of existence. In their respective liaisons with the erotically feminized forces of land and sea, Isaac and George live, however fleetingly, at fever pitch. If the price of momentary bliss is (at least for Isaac) one's immortal soul, then this sad denouement is also part and parcel of a misconceived Faustian bargain. In "Virility," Ozick rewrites the drama of transcendence by shifting the locus of ambition from nature to art. Her initial strategy is to invoke the theme of amibition by setting the story of Edmund Gate (né Elia Gatoff) to the familiar rhythm of the rags-to-riches scenario. Like the successful heroes of countless immigrant sages, Gate has fled Czarist Russia by way of Liverpool, finally to reach America, the promised land. Friendless, penniless, intellectually unprepossessing, he is armed for success only with *chutzpah* (brashness) that takes the form of self-confidence as unflagging as it is apparently unjustified. Despite his rudimentary English and lack of discernible talent, Gate channels his amibition into the writing of poetry. As he memorizes pages of the dictionary to perfect his English, Gate works at a succession of menial jobs for a newspaper, all the while turning out poetry. Awkward and contrived, his many poems testify only to his belief in hard work and the limitless possibilities of America. Yet after several years of predictable failure, his writing miraculously improves. Published in the best journals, collected in a first volume (*Virility*), and universally acclaimed by critics, Gate's poems earn him worldwide fame as unbelievable as it is sudden. With the publication of succeeding volumes (*Virility II–V*) Gate attains celebrity status, lecturing all over the world and drawing audiences three times the size of Caruso's. In Gate's inexorably linear progress from Russia to America, from ridicule to praise, from obscurity to fame, Ozick incarnates the immigrant's wildest dreams of worldly success.

So arbitrary yet inevitable is Gate's transformation from nonentity into genius that his career threatens to satirize the very set of conventions it embodies. Thus the rags-to-riches genre is radically destabilized by the central unbelievability of casting Gate's success not in the usual entrepreneurial but in aesthetic terms. The nearly half of "Virility" that chronicles Gate's apotheosis from all-but-unlettered immigrant to latter-day Keats (complete with death at twenty-six) is predominantly comic. Gate fires off dozens of poems at a time to a hodgepodge of periodicals—a "pastoral verse in earthy trochees" to a Vegetarian Party publication; "fragile dactyls on the subject of corsets" to the "organ of a ladies' tonic manufacturing firm" (242)—all of which are summarily rejected. Clichés encrusting the poet's persona—the blind faith in personal destiny, the laughably desperate efforts to publish, the exaggeratedly Rabelaisian life style—conspire to highlight (and thus to subvert) the greatest cliché of all: the meteoric rise to mastery and hence to fame. The cumulative effect of these deliberate commonplaces is to call into question not only the basis of Gate's fame but the nature of fame itself. In "Virility" fame turns out to be as much the product of critical consensus and public credulity as of poetic substance. As a sardonic commentary on the more than occasional disparity between aesthetic worth and critical and public acceptance, "Virility" may reflect Ozick's own experience. Her early stories "took years and years to find publication and some recognition." "The Pagan Rabbi," for example, "was finally published three or four years after its composition. . . . Each story had to battle for publication. . . . I have never recovered from early neglect. Who does?"[3]

If the unanimous praise that eluded Ozick but elevates Gate is suspiciously capricious in the rags-to-riches first movement of "Virility," it is unmistakably absurd in the sequel. When it turns out that Tante Rivka, the spinster aunt with whom Gate lived briefly in Liverpool, is the only true begetter of "his" poems, Ozick's satiric targets multiply. Exploded along with the *idiot savant* myth that purportedly accounted for Gate's success are the adulatory critical opinions which fashioned his reputation. Reviewers who hailed the "superbly controlled muscle" of Gate's "masculine poems" (257) dismiss the collection that, published under Tante Rivka's name, contains her finest poems as "thin feminine art," the products of a "spinster's one-dimensional vision" (266). Ozick's point is that critical opinion—overwhelmingly male—is biased in favor of the masculine and against the feminine. *Flowers from Liverpool* receives the critics' kiss of death because of its title and "pretty cover, the color of a daisy's petal, with a picture of Tante Rivka on it" (264). In "Previsions of the Demise of the Dancing Dog," an essay originally published in the same year (1971) as "Virility," Ozick forges the same link between literary criticism and sexist bias. Teaching English in a large urban university, Ozick is struck by the fact that "both my students and my colleagues were equal adherents of the Ovarian Theory of Literature, or, rather, its complement, the Testicular Theory."[4] When she assigns Flannery O'Connor's *Wise Blood,* her students, initially astonished to learn that a woman had written this violent and hard-edged novel, quickly take refuge in sexist stereotyping, arguing with no more intelligence than Tante Rivka's detractors that

O'Connor "*sounds* like a woman—she has to sound that way because she is."[5] In their sexist rush to judgment, Ozick goes on to argue, the students emulate reviewers: "I think I can say in good conscience that I have never— repeat, *never*—read a review of a novel or, especially, of a collection of poetry by a woman that did not include somewhere in its columns a gratuitous allusion to the writer's sex and its supposed effects."[6] In "Virility," Edmund Gate's last words to the narrator—"I'm a man"—spoken while clutching his testicles and after he has confessed his plagiarism constitute a pathetically ironic recourse to masculinity as a counter to poetic impotence.

"Envy; or, Yiddish in America" also concerns the practice of poetry. At its center stands the sixty- seven-year-old Yiddish poet Hershel Edelshtein, con- demned to write in a dying language for a diminishing audience. "Whoever uses Yiddish to keep himself alive is already dead" (67), mourns Edelshtein to Paula, the wife of Baumzweig, whose aptly named journal *Bitterer Yam* (*Bitter Sea*) is the sole outlet for Edelshtein's poetry. Yid- dish, murdered in Europe by the Holocaust and spurned by Israel in favor of Hebrew, survives only tenuously in America. Because American-born Jews prefer assimila- tion to distinctiveness, the universal to the parochial— hence English to Yiddish—Edelshtein's already minuscule audience will soon disappear. And because Edelshtein (and Ozick) views Yiddish as a crucial aspect of Jewish- ness, his struggle to preserve a language is also a struggle to preserve a history. At the 1970 American-Israeli Dia- logue, Ozick delivered an address which may be read not only as a gloss on the linguistic and cultural issues raised in "Envy" but as a statement of her personal aesthetic. Published as an essay entitled "America: Toward

Yavneh,'' the address followed less than a year after the original publication date (November 1969) of "Envy." In the essay Ozick calls for a "Jewish liturgical literature written in English" but constituting a kind of "New Yiddish."[7] By means of this "centrally Jewish" form of writing (e.g., "Envy") Jewish culture, all but wiped out in the Holocaust, may survive and even flourish in the American diaspora. What must be resisted is the impulse—all too common among American Jews—"to give ourselves over altogether to Gentile culture and be lost to history."[8]

While the decrepitude of Edelshtein—and Baumzweig—dramatizes the predicament of Yiddish in modern America, Edelshtein himself is far from an ideal champion of Jewish cultural values. True, he strives to keep Yiddish alive by lecturing to Americanized Jews in their garish new temples. But even as he seems to mourn the death of Yiddish, he actually mourns the dwindling of an audience and the consequent future irrelevance of his own poetry. His desperate search for a translator reflects, therefore, not only his hunger for literary fame but his fear of impending literary death. Widowed, childless, nearly friendless, the aging Edelshtein sees in translation his only hope of immortality, the only proof of his earthly existence. In his pleading letter to Hannah, a twenty-three-year-old Yiddish adept and his last hope of finding a translator, Edelshtein self-servingly equates his personal fate with the fate of Yiddish, and even of the Jewish people. While Edelshtein's argument—that the "twelve million people . . . who lived inside this tongue" were halved by the Holocaust and that "whoever forgets Yiddish courts amnesia of history" (74)—is unassailable, his conclusion—that translating his poetry into English is an act of linguistic and historical redemption—is dubious. Translation cannot, after all, preserve a language, only its texts. And translating worthless texts may actually dishonor or trivialize the very language and history it evokes. Arguing that preserving his poetry preserves Yiddish, Edelshtein begs the question of the viability of that poetry. But whatever his poetry's merit, Edelshtein's hypocrisy does not blind him to the real motives underlying his appeal to Hannah. Breaking the letter off in mid-sentence, he admits that in mourning the dead he mourns himself: "His cry was ego and more ego. . . . He wanted someone to read his poems. . . . Filth and exploitation to throw in history" (75). In mercilessly refusing to breathe life into Edelshtein's poems, Hannah senses the hypocrisy in his desperation. But in the contempt of her refusal, she diminishes herself more than Edelshtein. Repudiating Jewish suffering, referring to "you people" and "you Jews," Hannah distances herself—and the American-born Jewish youth she represents—from the "old men from the ghetto," personified by Edelshtein. While it may be true that Edelshtein's increasingly shrill pleas for translation reveal not so much commitment to the language and history of the Jews as ambition for fame among the Gentiles, he has merely abused Jewish history. Hannah would cancel it: "History's a waste" (92).

Underlying Hannah's attack on Edelshtein is her (and her generation's) sacrifice of the parochial (Jewish) for the universal (humanity). Although her Yiddish background ostensibly belies her disaffection, she has undergone a sort of reverse conversion. Separating herself from Jewish history, she melts anonymously into the world at large. That world is often invoked as the object of desire, the locus of ambition for Yiddishists like Edelshtein who aspire to a greater audience than their language affords. The action of "Envy" takes place almost exlusively within the tight confines of the New York Yiddish community, itself an embodiment of the constrictions imposed by a dying language. Only Yankel Ostrover among the Yiddishists has gained the wider recognition that they all, with varying degress of envy, desire. And only Ostrover, a thinly disguised caricature of Isaac Bashevis Singer, has been freed from the "prison of Yiddish" by virtue of translation. For the jealous Edelshtein—and others—Ostrover's success stems neither from the grace of his style ("impure," "vile") nor the profundity of his subject matter ("pornographic," "freakish"), but from his translators. Ironically, it may be that the very form and content reviled by Yiddish purists account for Ostrover's/Singer's fame "in the world of reality," where he is considered a "modern."

If the Ostrover of "Envy" were a literary hack and Edelshtein an authentic talent born to blush unseen, the story would be about the exigencies of translation. In this scenario luck alone accounts for the former's fame, the latter's obscurity. This Edelshtein believes, but his belief is ill-founded, and the tenacity with which he holds it renders him sporadically comic. Equally comic is his oscillation between the personae of fearful *shtetl* Jew and fearless arbiter of Yiddish culture. Most comic of all is his hypocritical frenzy to emulate the very success he debunks. As if to emphasize the comicality—and the banality—of Edelshtein's motivation, Ozick throws in a passing reference to a long-ago affair between Ostrover and Edelshtein's wife. Yet Ozick's full title resists classifying Edelshtein solely as the incarnation of envy. For he is at the same time the personification of Yiddish in

America and of Jewish history in general. The conclusion of "Envy" flows directly from Hannah's virulent attack on Edelshtein when she refuses to translate his poetry, calling him irrelevant not only for Gentiles but even for Jews. The nearly anti-Semitic tone of her denunciation expresses her (and her generation's?) radical disengagement from "old Jews" such as Edelshtein. Edelshtein, in turn, is staggered by the irony of the situation: that a young Jewish woman, miraculously speaking Yiddish, seems bent on annihilating the very tradition she seems born to preserve. Already marginalized by the Holocaust, that tradition is further debilitated by the disaffection of its putative adherents—the forgetful old and the indifferent young. Driven into a corner by Hannah's invective, Edelshtein admits that his ideas are used up, his poetry imitative; his last plea for translation is simply that of an old man. As such he attains representative status, not as mediocre Yiddish poet but as waning Jewish elder. Attacking Edelshtein, Hannah attacks the Jewish history she scorns; her "victory" suggests closure—of his life, of that history.

With Hannah's more than symbolic words of murder—"Die now, all you old men . . . the whole bunch of you, parasites, hurry up and die" (97)—still ringing in his ears, Edelshtein flees her presence. The setting of their climactic encounter—her uncle Vorovsky's apartment—like the story's other main locales—the 92nd Street Y, Baumzweig's apartment—reflects the insularity of Yiddish New York. By confining the action of "Envy" largely to the minuscule community of Yiddishists, Ozick achieves tragicomic nuances analogous to those in Edelshtein's makeup. On the one hand, Edelshtein's dilemma is a tempest in a teapot; but on the other, its ripples reflect the greater dilemmas facing the Yiddish language and Jewish culture. Between major scenes played out with fellow Yiddishists of varying stripes and conflicting persuasions, Edelshtein walks the streets of New York. These constitute less a coherent site than an evocation of the larger (Gentile) society which necessarily impinges upon the tight little Yiddish island it surrounds. All but cast by Hannah into this outer world, Edelshtein hears her slurs redoubled—and restated in the rabid language of anti-Semitism—during the bizarre telephone conversation that concludes "Envy." Underlying this comically exaggerated exchange of insults between Jew and anti-Semite (the story's only Gentile voice) is the same terror of annihilation that provoked Edelshtein's search for a translator. Edelshtein's last words—shouted over the telephone to the anti-Semite—blame his unseen tormentor for his fate: "On account of you I lost everything, my whole life! On account of you I have no translator!" (100). In this close juxtaposition of literary and actual death lies the most striking proof that translation is in "Envy" a metaphor for existence. As poet—and Jew—Edelshtein has been denied the fullness of life by the opposing cultural values of the Gentile world, values which have claimed and corrupted Hannah and made her the agent of his downfall. That Edelshtein is no ideal embodiment of the Yiddish poet or the Jewish people is a crucial factor in the story. For Hannah and the Jewish youth she represents it is easy to concur with the Gentiles who constitute mainstream American culture in praising an Ostrover. Far more difficult is it apparently for these same Jews to preserve and protect an Edelshtein. In deafening herself to his pleas, Hannah allies herself with the Gentiles—even the anti-Semites—who would honor the one Jew at he expense of the many. Initially a comic symbol of the poet victimized by his own lack of talent, Edelshtein becomes finally a tragic symbol of the Jew victimized by the indifference of his coreligionists and the contempt of the Gentiles.

Unlike Edelshtein, a Jew among Jews in "Envy," Genevieve is the lone Jew in the radically different setting of "The Suitcase": the New York art world. The confrontation between Jew and Gentile—and their respective ethos—confined to a single telephone conversation in "Envy," makes up the central action of "The Suitcase." Edelshtein's bitter exchange of epithets with the anti-Semite is anticlimactic in the sense that it confirms what was already known; Genevieve's politely destructive exchange with Mr. Hencke is climactic in the sense that it reveals what was only suspected. Like Edelshtein, Genevieve is cast as representative Jew—but one whose victimization is less immediately apparent than his. Although Mr. Hencke, a former pilot in the Kaiser's air force, has lived in America so long that he "no longer thought of himself as a German" (103), he is forced by Genevieve into a role as symbolic as her own. Mr. Hencke correctly interprets her comparison of the people crowded together at Gottfried's exhibit to concentration camp victims and of Gottfried's paintings to "shredded swastikas" as an attempt to label him a "Nazi sympathizer even now, an anti-Semite, an Eichmann" (109). If it is true that Genevieve tries to make of Mr. Hencke the stereotypical German, it is equally true that he makes of her the stereotypical Jew—"the sort who, twenty years after Hitler's war, would not buy a Volkswagen, . . . full of detestable moral gestures" (109). It seems to Mr. Hencke that Genevieve's "detestable moral gestures" are misdirected and that he, a man who has "harmed no one," is a victim of Jewish revenge.

To accept Mr. Hencke's point of view is to read "The Suitcase" as a study in reverse victimization: "Genevieve as Jew is a victim, but in the story it is Mr. Hencke who is victimized, reduced from strength and self assurance to uncertaintly and tearful guilt."[9] But this is to confuse revelation with victimization. Only in the narrow sense of being prodded into an unconscious admission of guilt can Mr. Hencke be regarded as a victim. His compulsive show of innocence—when Genevieve's purse is stolen he throws "open his suitcase with so much wild vigor that it quivered on its hinges" (126)—is the guilty reflex of a man whose innate Germanness has just been exposed. His extravagant denial—"Please, I swear it"—of a petty crime against a Jew, which of course he did not commit, is actually a denial of his complicity as a German (and possibly an anti-Semite) in the massive crimes committed against all Jews. Mr. Hencke insists to Genevieve that his suitcase is packed for Sweden, not for Germany—"I swear it"—juxtaposing the innocence of the Swedes, who "saved so many Jews," with his own innocence as regards the missing purse. It is largely by means of such ironic juxtapositions, clustering together in the last few pages of "The Suitcase," that Mr. Hencke in protesting too much aligns himself with the victimizers. And it is impossible to read Catherine's joke about the "criminals we've harbored unawares!"—which "sounded exactly like a phrase of Genevieve's" (127)—as anything but a shatteringly ironic reference to Mr. Hencke.

To see Mr. Hencke as a victim is to conspire with him in obliterating the history he would prefer to forget or at least subtly to revise. As a Jew, Genevieve can condone neither his amnesia nor his revisionism. She therefore strips away the American veneer to expose the German foundation of Mr. Hencke's identity. For him the Holocaust was perpetrated not by Germans but by the impersonal forces of history: "Who could be blamed for History?" which "was a Force-in-Itself, like Evolution" (109). "A horrible tragedy," he calls his sister's loss of home and daughter of eleven in an R.A.F. raid on Cologne. Yet he is silent about the infinitely more horrible tragedy of the Holocaust that engulfed six million Jews. Aside from that suffered by his sister, the only other "tragedy" he sees fit to mention is the damage sustained by the Cologne cathedral. To Genevieve's remark that if Jung were a Jewish psychiatrist (as Catherine had mistakenly thought) he would have been murdered by the Nazis, Mr. Hencke replies, "Everybody dies." This bland rejoinder, effectively equating natural process and genocide, is among the most striking of Mr. Hencke's evasive strategies. By successively exposing—and exploding—these strategies, Genevieve forces upon Mr. Hencke the awareness of his implication in the atrocities. To dismiss, to depersonalize, to universalize those atrocities is to commit further atrocity oneself. Toward the end of "The Suitcase" Holocaust imagery—smoke from German chimneys, coat "scorched into gray" (127)—invokes history to override Mr. Hencke's pleas of innocence. No Eichmann, Mr. Hencke nonetheless reveals symptoms of what the distinguished Jewish political philosopher Hannah Arendt saw revealed in that infamous Nazi war criminal: the banality of evil.

If Mr. Hencke's inauthenticity consists of evading history, Dr. Silver's consists of evading life itself. On the eve of his fiftieth birthday the antihero of "The Doctor's Wife" looks back upon a life distinguished chiefly by what he had not done. "At twenty he had endured the

stunned emotion of one who senses that he has been sin-
gled out for aspiration, for beauty, for awe, for some par-
ticularity not yet disclosed'' (187–88). Still ''without a
history'' at forty, he ''began to despise himself because he
had put his faith in the possibility of significant, of miraculous, event'' (188). In this shock of recognition Dr. Silver grasps not only the root of his error but the means of
his redemption. Unfortunately, his decision to marry
comes too late, so that he falls in love ''as men of that
age will, with a picture.'' Failing to achieve redemption in
marriage, Dr. Silver seeks redemption in art. Perhaps conditioned by the banal marriages of his sisters—he ''did
not differentiate among the sisters or their husbands''
(176)—Dr. Silver prefers union with a portrait to marriage
with a woman. Portrait *becomes* woman in Dr. Silver's
conversion of the anonymous figure in the photograph into
his wife and the mother of his children as a ploy for dis-
posing of Miss Steinweh. Already fifty, Dr. Silver creates
a fictitious family as the ultimate rejection of an actual
one, thus finalizing his flight from life into art.

The picture appears in a biography of Chekhov, who, as
Dr. Silver notes, ''was also a doctor, a bachelor up to the
last minute'' (188). In the stories and plays of Chekhov,
the Russian master whose influence on Ozick is exceeded
only by that of James, the bachelor doctor is a recurring
figure. Generally intelligent, observant, detached, realistic
if not sardonic, Chekhov's doctors are habitually—and often simplistically—identifed with Chekhov himself. And
Chekhov is regarded—again simplistically—as the por-
trayer par excellence of futility, boredom, stasis. To the
extent that many of Chekhov's characters fail to act and
that relatively little happens in his works, Dr. Silver might
be a Chekhovian character, ''The Doctor's Wife'' a Chek-

hovian story. Dr. Silver's identification with Chekhov and appropriation of the unknown woman from Chekhov's biography are only the most overt signs of Chekhov's presence in "The Doctor's Wife." The final movement of Ozick's story, for example, recapitulates a typical Chekhovian situation of unfulfilled promise. At the conclusion of *The Cherry Orchard,* Chekhov's last play, the anticipated marriage of Lopakhin and Varya comes to nothing. Varya, forsaken by Lopakhin, is, like Gerda Steinweh forsaken by Dr. Silver, condemned to spinsterhood: Miss Steinweh, muses Dr. Silver, "was a sunset, it was the last hour before her night, the warmth of her last youth was ebbing, she was at the excruciating fulcrum of transition" (203).

That moment of transition occurred for Dr. Silver years earlier when he fell in love with a picture captioned "Unknown Friend" in the Chekhov biography. Still—like so many Chekhov characters—he remains capable of self-delusion: "His life now was only a temporary accommodation, he was young, he was preparing for the future, he would beget progeny, . . . his most intense capacities, his deepest consummations, lay ahead" (182–83). Paradoxically, the photograph both dispels and sustains such fantasies. The locus of Dr. Silver's sublimated desires and therefore the burial site of his illusions, it is at the same time the most extravagant of his illusions, the greatest self-deception of all. Self-delusion, repression, sublimation are typically Chekhovian, as is the flickering awareness of the pathology of evasion. Thus Dr. Silver understands that the photograph is "deeply perilous," and resolves to discard it along with his other illusions: "All the photographs of the mind—out! All the photographs of hope and self-deception—out!" (189). What distinguishes

Dr. Silver from his Chekhovian counterparts is his essential coldness. Arriving late for his own birthday party, greeted with shrieks, laughter, applause, music, kisses, and cries of "Happy Birthday!" and "Speech!" the doctor remains "unmoved, hiding his coldness" (198). As always, he is revolted by the spectacle of quotidian life, disgusted by its sloppiness and clamor. Chekhov's characters, too, most often fail to achieve or to sustain meaningful relationships with their fellow human beings. Futile, immobile, they can barely articulate their deeply felt yearnings for union. But Dr. Silver feels nothing. Never does he express love for another person, only universal contempt—for his father; for his sisters and their husbands and children; for his patients. Even Chekhov's most aloof doctors are not uncaring. Indeed, their air of bemused detachment is often a smoke screen for caring too much. What Chekhov's doctors feel is rooted in experience; what Dr. Silver does not feel results from evading experience.

Dr. Silver's withdrawal from experience culminates in the family fiction he confides to Gerda Steinweh. Woven about the unidentified woman friend of Chekhov, the spurious narrative represents his farthest flight from the reality he abhors. Dr. Silver's escape—not just from Miss Steinweh but from the life she represents—is as deliberate as it is far-fetched. Fully conscious of opting for the illusion he once had explicitly rejected, Dr. Silver eschews the risks of life for the safety of art. That Dr. Silver twice claims to be happy in the willed sterility that produces only fictional children and distances him from humanity is an ironic comment on his definition of, and capacity for, happiness. His family narrative concluded, the doctor watches Miss Steinweh, who "looked kind," dancing with one of his brothers-in-law. Ever the watcher, never the dancer, Dr. Silver, in erecting his narrative barrier against the kind Miss Steinweh (she is, ironically, a guidance counselor), attains the living death that Chekhov's characters struggle, however ineffectually, to escape. It is, however, within a distinctly un-Chekhovian mise-en-scène that Dr. Silver chooses to become a Chekhovian character. Because the life teeming around him is anything but static, Dr. Silver would be more at home in a Chekhov story than in his own. Chekhov's characters grope toward or pirouette around one another, only to fall short or to drift apart. Unable to attain—or even fully to articulate— their heart's desires, they settle into passivity and ultimate immobility. It is exactly this petrifaction that awaits Dr. Silver: his story of an imaginary wife does not so much release the unknown woman from the photograph as imprison himself within it.

NOTES

1. Ozick, *Art and Ardor* (New York: Knopf, 1983) 169.

2. Ozick, *The Pagan Rabbi and Other Stories* (New York: Knopf, 1971) 217. Page references in parentheses are to this edition.

3. Catherine Rainwater and William J. Scheick, "An Interview with Cynthia Ozick (Summer 1982)," *Texas Studies in Literature and Language* 25 (Summer 1983) 257.

4. *Art and Ardor* 266.

5. *Art and Ardor* 267.

6. *Art and Ardor* 268.

7. *Art and Ardor* 176. Here the essay is reprinted as "Toward a New Yiddish," 154–77.

8. *Art and Ardor* 177.

9. Josephine Z. Knopp, "The Jewish Stories of Cynthia Ozick," *Studies in American Jewish Literature*, 1 (1975) 35.

CHAPTER FOUR

Bloodshed and Three Novellas and *The Shawl*

By the time of *Bloodshed and Three Novellas* (1976) Ozick had completed the transition from American novelist to Jewish storyteller already apparent in *The Pagan Rabbi and Other Stories.* Questions of Jewish identity— its matrices, its manifestations, ultimately its meanings— relatively muted in *Trust,* come to dominate the short fiction. "Bloodshed," for example, focuses on a key aspect of Jewishness: the responsibilities conferred on American Jews by the Holocaust and the extent to which such responsibilities set Jews apart from others. The title strongly suggests that it is the immemorial spilling of Jewish blood, culminating in the unspeakable atrocities of the Holocaust, that unites—or should unite—Jew with Jew. Just as all Jews stood symbolically together at Sinai, they suffered symbolically together during the Nazi conflagration. In each of the fictions in *Bloodshed and Three Novellas* Jewish identity is betrayed.[1] But in "An Education" the betrayal of Jewish identity, no less egregious than in the other stories, is least crucial to its outcome.

Names reflect the unstable identities of the chief Jewish characters. Una, a non-Jewish name lifted from the stories of the Irish Catholic Frank O'Connor, may also refer to the Una of Book 1 of Edmund Spenser's Renaissance Protestant epic, *The Faerie Queene*. Hers is an unambiguous identity (the One) in Spenser. When it is combined with a Jewish last name (Meyer), the effect in "An Education" is to blur rather than to clarify Una's identity. Moreover, Ozick's Una is "one" only in her lack of complexity; the greater part of the story depends upon the unrelieved simplicity of her one-dimensional character. Unlike Una Meyer, whose pallid Jewishness is inherited and largely unconscious, the married couple who literally, and figuratively, take her in have taken pains to de-Judaize themselves. Their devalued lives are symbolized by a change in names: from Chaims (Hebrew for "life") to Chimes ("like what a bell does"). They ostentatiously eat ham, name their daughter Christina, and are pro-Arab on the Israeli question. Clement Chimes even makes light of the definitive Jewish tragedy, punning on Holy Ghost/Holocaust. In the sort of retributive denouement that marks much of Ozick's post-*Trust* fiction, Christina dies and Clement's "masterwork"—the fancifully titled "Social Cancer/A Diagnosis in Verse/And Anger"—never gets written.

While Clement Chimes registers as a near-comic caricature of the Jew-hating Jew—he even attends Union Theological Seminary—the Chimeses deracination and its consequences is not the true subject of "An Education." To maintain that the story's "central theme" is "the cultural vacuum which ensues when they try to integrate themselves within the Gentile majority," and that Clement "fails because, having renounced his Jewish birthright, he faces the dilemma of trying to write literature without any cultural roots whatsoever" would be accurate only if "An

Education'' were the Chimeses' story.[2] The Chimeses' deracination seems more misanthropic than integrative. Its effect—isolation rather than affiliation—is sought deliberately as evidence of their own exclusiveness. Theirs is not the religion of the Gentiles but of Beauty, chiefly their own: narcissistic, selfish, manipulative, they enlist naïve young women, first Rosalie, later Una, as acolytes at the altar of their self-worship. They reserve their bitterest scorn for those who, like Rosalie, defect from their worship or who, like Organski, disdain it. This said, it is not the Chimeses per se but their impact on Una that is central to ''An Education.'' Indeed the Chimeses disappear from the story's last episode, leaving Una to absorb and assess the meaning of her liaison with them. ''An Education'' is finally Una's story: the Chimeses are her educators, hers the education.

Una's initial education is narrowly academic. A classics graduate student, she need only write her dissertation—on left-handed Etruscan goddesses in Southern Turkey—to complete her PhD. The dissertation topic, reflecting academic triviality and pretense, holds no apparent interest or relevance for Una. At twenty-four Una is the same innocent and ordinary girl she was at eighteen. Intellectually and sexually cloistered, she is an easy mark for exploitation. Enter the Chimeses—and Henry James. That James's ghost hovers over ''An Education'' is not surprising. At seventeen, says Ozick, she had already fallen ''into the jaws of James'' by virtue of a first reading of ''The Beast in the Jungle.''[3] Her MA thesis, ''Parable in the Late Novels of Henry James''; her several essays on ''the only American writer whom our well-ingrained democratic literary conventions have been willing to call 'Master' '';[4] and her many acknowledgments of his influ-

ence—for better or for worse—on her fiction attest to
Ozick's career-long obsession with James. Even her preference for writing novellas, while not explicitly credited
to his influence, predictably alludes to James: "I never
sought it out, as James did, because I thought it was
'blest.' "[5] The morality, scrupulosity, ambiguity, and
irony that define James's fiction are equally critical to
Ozick's. What makes "An Education" the most Jamesian
of her stories is its seamless interweaving of the Master's
aesthetic with his quintessential dramatic situation.

There is, of course, nothing uniquely Jamesian about
the drama of initiation, but it is developed by Ozick along
familiar Jamesian lines. Even before those lines are established, the Master's presence is invoked in Una's initial
visit to the Chimeses' apartment. Prowling among their
books, she first notices "the entire original New York
edition of Henry James." A few months later, when Mary
Chimes gives birth to a daughter, the baby is named
Christina "after the heroine of *The Princess Casamas-
sima*," a James novel. As the initiation motif jells, the
affinity between its treatment in "An Education" and in
specific fictions of James becomes more pronounced. A
favorite James device is to trace the arc of a protagonist's
gathering awareness not only of his/her own role but of
the larger human drama in which he or she is a role-
player. Stories such as "The Pupil," "The Lesson of the
Master," "The Beast in the Jungle," and "The Real
Thing"—like "An Education"—treat initiation as consequent upon exploitation. "The Pupil" is the James story
that in its situation and character relationships seems most
likely to have inspired "An Education." In both stories a
knowing and selfish couple plays upon an innocent and
selfless young person. Like the tutor in "The Pupil," Una

opens herself to endless exploitation by forming a close attachment to a child. James's charming but conniving couple has identically exploited previous tutors by delaying and finally reneging on their pay. Ozick's far less charming but no less conniving Chimeses, having already made maximum use of Rosalie, "befriend" Una by allowing her to pay a large portion of their rent; to do their shopping, cooking, and cleaning; to provide secretarial help for Clement and child care for Christina; even to contribute her meager salary from working nights at a hardware store to their household. Neither James nor Ozick exonerates the exploiting couple, but both hint strongly that the protagonist who follows false gods is partly culpable. Even more than James's tutor, Una begins by idolizing the victimizers, whom she naïvely associates with truth and beauty. This note of self-victimization through self-deception, so often struck by James, reverberates as well in "An Education."

While "The Lesson of the Master" and "The Beast in the Jungle" have fewer points of correspondence with "An Education" than does "The Pupil," they too treat aspects of initiation that recur in Ozick's story. The Master's hypocritical exhortation to live only for Art that costs Paul Overt his fiancée ("The Lesson of the Master") takes the form of the Chimeses' equally self-serving advice about solving "the problem of the Self" that costs Una her Fulbright grant. "An Education" follows "The Lesson of the Master" by deploying deceitful but convincing gurus falsely to signpost the path of initiation. In "The Beast in the Jungle" Marcher's self-deception (imagining himself destined for a special fate, he passes the better part of his life conjecturing about its nature and awaiting its occurrence) leads to a wasted life and ultimate loneliness. Una wastes months, not years. Her epiphany of loss is far less devastating and her eventual loneliness far more self-willed (she refuses Organski's repeated offers of marriage) than Marcher's. But she shares Marcher's mistaken sense of destiny and belated self-knowledge.

With the death of Christina—the transcendent embodiment of the Chimeses "beauty"—and the consequent flight of the Chimeses, Una is ostensibly released from their spell. She goes on to finish her PhD, writing a dissertation that "required no travel, foreign or internal," and never seeing the Chimeses again. So profound, however, has been their influence that ultimately Una can neither forget nor condemn them. Unlike Rosalie, who never forgives the Chimeses, Una believes that "they had something, . . . they kept themselves intact. They had *that*." For Una the Chimeses, revealed in all their shallowness and selfishness, nonetheless possessed a singular unity: "They're the only persons I've ever known who stayed the same from start to finish" (126). From the Chimeses, "authentic" in their fashion, Una learns lessons more personal than aesthetic. Organski attributes her refusal to marry him—or anyone—to her unflagging belief in the perfection of the Chimeses' marriage. He sees her as traumatized by the fear that she can never duplicate that perfect union which she had vicariously lived. Even if Organski's marriage-trauma theory is partially or wholly wrong (a sop to his vanity, a salve for his frustration), he may be right about the ultimate effect on Una of her life with the Chimeses. As richly ambiguous as its Jamesian analogues, the ending of "An Education" likewise supports multiple interpretations. Una at forty-two seems still to shy away from experience, whether owing to or reacting against the example of the Chimeses. Accordingly, the girl who was the same at twenty-four (and at forty-two?)

as she had been at eighteen, "lived" only in that brief interstice of her life which she spent with the Chimeses. Yet the brief life scenario must take into account the novella's final sentence: "It wasn't that she any longer resented imperfection, but it seemed to her unendurable that her education should go on and on and on." Una "who waited a decade before she dared to visit them," has just left the house of Boris and Rosalie: the Organskis' "house held no glory and no wars." Una's aloneness is, after all, self-willed, the product of her long-ago brush with the "real thing." That isolation might as easily represent a courageous refusal (à la militant feminism) knowingly to settle for the patent imperfection of the Organskis' marriage. Una's education—"unendurable" but plainly endured—may evidence not the closure of the self but the self's endless exfoliation in knowledge.

Although the characters in "An Education" are all Jews, and Jewish deracination marks the inauthentic, the terms of Una's initiation are not specifically Jewish. Compared to stories in which Jewishness is the litmus test of true knowledge and thus the sole determinant of successful initiation, "An Education" seems inconclusive, deliberately ambiguous. Ozick gives no indication that Una's initiation is contingent upon degrees of Jewishness. Applied solely to the Chimeses, the litmus test of Jewishness is only one aspect of the larger issue of the genuine versus the phony that dominates "An Education." And the issue remains in the end clouded: Una recognizes the inauthenticity of the Chimeses' actions even as she maintains the authenticity of their identities.

Of course Una may mistake mere consistency, no matter how banal or destructive, for authenticity. In "A Mercenary" no such confusion is possible: Lushinski is inauthentic precisely because he has disclaimed Jewishness. Jewish deracination—comic in the Chimeses—is tragic in Lushinski. The deeper note of "A Mercenary" is struck immediately in an epigraph attributed to Joseph Goebbels, Hitler's infamous propagandist: "Today we are all expressionists—men who want to make the world outside themselves take the form of their life within themselves." Goebbels's words are characteristically sinister in their historical context, implying that the Holocaust— that definitive "creation" of Nazi "expressionism"—reflected the twisted lives of its perpetrators. German expressionists depicted not objective reality but the subjective emotions and responses that objects and events aroused in the artist. While expressionism predates Hitler's Third Reich, the expressionist aesthetic of distortion prefigures the Nazi wrenchings of German culture, values, even language to conform to a twisted world view. In varying degrees Lushinski and the two other main characters of "A Mercenary" have reinvented themselves, thereby altering their relationship to the world. Seemingly a relatively innocuous form of distortion, the destabilized identity is nonetheless symptomatic of a more general chaos that Jews have learned by bitter experience to dread.

Stanislav Lushinski, the mercenary of the title, has turned himself inside out in every conceivable fashion. A Polish Jew, he has long represented a small unnamed black African country at the United Nations. He has exchanged his cold and gray European homeland for hot and bright Africa, his native language for tribal dialect and diplomat's English, his Judaism for cosmopolitanism. Lushinski is most at home in New York, the quintessential melting pot where identities are confused, altered, reinvented. Still, he is essentially homeless even in New York, traveling incessantly around the United States and returning to Africa only sporadically and then mainly for official visits. Even his sexual identity is fluid: he lives with a mistress, Louisa (Lulu), in New York; with an Italian boy in Geneva. Lushinski crafts his public persona on the television talk shows (the ultimate symbol of the ephemeral?) on which he delights to appear. That his life is in good part a fairy tale of his own telling is underlined in Ozick's ''Once upon a time'' lead-in to one of Lushinski's many television appearances. A consummate actor, he loves the cameras which record his performances and the studio audiences who love his stories. Mocking, parodic, contradictory, his tales are reminiscent of the patter of standup comedians who nightly redo themselves. Joking about his past becomes a strategy for effacing it: ''He had made himself over, and now he was making himself up''(28).

Morris Ngambe, Lushinski's young assistant, and Louisa, his mistress, have likewise made themselves over, albeit not so thoroughly or so consciously. A black African only a couple of generations removed from the bush, Morris has acquired the manner and manners of an English gentleman by virtue of an Oxford education. In so doing he has reversed the de-Europeanizing trajectory of Lushinski: ''A Mercenary'' ends with Morris in New York (''a city of Jews''), Lushinski in black Africa. Louisa, reputedly a former German countess whose last name was preceded by a ''von,'' seems thoroughly American. But her accent—''a fake melody either Irish or Swedish'' (21)—belies both identities, German and American. Louisa claims to have ''once run a famous chemical corporation in California'' but to have given up everything for

Lushinski. In the three central characters of "A Mercenary," Ozick has calibrated identity transformed, from the case of Louisa, who seems essentially American, her German origins hazy and glossed over; to that of Morris, whose African past is never fully subsumed under a European patina; finally to that of Lushinski, whose metamorphosis from Polish Jew into cosmopolitan mercenary (by definition a metamorphic calling) is both more conscious and more thorough than the changes wrought in themselves by Louisa and Morris.

Least conscious of multiple identities because least burdened by history is Louisa. But Morris and Lushinski, shadowed respectively by African colonialism and European Holocaust, cannot so easily escape their pasts. In New York, despite his Oxford degree, Morris suffers like any black: he is snubbed and sent to the service entrance of a Riverside Drive apartment by a Puerto Rican elevator man; he is patronized and ignored by the Secretary of State who pays attention only to Lushinski; and he is knocked down and robbed by a gang of youths whose windbreakers ironically read "Africa First, Harlem Nowhere." That Morris's acquired persona begins to chafe is evidenced by his suddenly tight underwear, his perspiration, and his growing hatred of New York, which he comes to see as less civilized, more a "jungle"" than his native Africa. His identity crisis comes to a head in his recollection of the Tarzan movies he once compulsively attended. Morris fears himself to be a self-duped mimic of Western manners, a black version of "that lout Tarzan" whose crude chatter parodies African dialect. Even more jarring to Morris's sense of himself is Roberto Rossellini's classic Italian film *General della Rovere* (1959). Vittorio De Sica plays a scruffy con man, a blowhard who impersonates a famous World War II military hero so successfully that he gradually takes on the general's moral stature, acting with genuine courage. There is, moreover, a subtextual doubling of the film's story of heroic impersonation: the middle-aged De Sica, a matinee idol as a young man, playfully mocks his former persona. For Morris, however, *General della Rovere's* theme of self-transcendence as a mode of personal discovery collapses into the same accommodation offered by the ferocious natives to Tarzan. Troubled by "the problem of sincerity," Morris worries that jumping into someone else's skin—which inevitably begins to fit—is to inhabit no culture. It is his revulsion against his perceived inauthenticity—"How long could the ingested, the invented, foreignness endure"—that drives Morris eventually to reverse Lushinski's direction, and to reclaim his African heritage.

Unlike Morris, Lushinski is untroubled by the question of sincerity. Symbolic of his many possible identities, any one of which he can assume at a moment's notice, are the several complete sets of false papers, passports, and diplomas he keeps in an "always reliably present" suitcase. Ever ready to exchange the life he has spun out on television for one no less arbitrarily conceived, Lushinski, the deracinated Jew, welcomes the very homelessness that for the real Jew is an endless affliction. He calls himself "the century's one free man" (37), not only because as a Holocaust survivor he has already experienced the worst that can happen to a human being but also because he is not imprisoned in a single identity. Having trivialized his own tragic past—and by extension the Holocaust—by reducing it to television patter, Lushinski has exorcised his former self and made all identities equally plausible. To Louisa, Lushinski denies "being part of the Jews," claiming rather to be "a part of mankind." It is exactly this sort of appeal to universalism that Ozick deplores in the last sentences of her 1970 essay "Toward a New Yiddish": "If we blow into the narrow end of the *shofar,* we will be heard far. But if we choose to be Mankind rather than Jewish and blow into the wider part, we will not be heard at all; for us America will have been in vain."[6] For Ozick Jewish assimilationism amounts to Jewish disappearance, the ironically macabre culmination in America of what Hitler began in Germany.

Still, despite claiming that "I am an African" and snubbing Jews at the United Nations Assembly, Lushinski is haunted by the vestigial remains of the Jew he was. Chief among these are the characteristically Jewish reliance on words and obsession with history. As a "paid mouthpiece" he has long corrupted words; as a talk-show guest he has relentlessly devalued history. But he is forced finally to confront words and history not in the shallow sense in which he has employed them but in the full resonance of their Jewish bearings. When Louisa calls Lushinski "You Jew," she "restored him to fear"—to the Jew he once was and, in some measure, must ever be. A word suffices to pierce the armor of Lushinski's painstakingly crafted public identity and expose the Jew beneath. The transcendent importance of words for Jews is forcefully expressed by Elie Wiesel, perhaps the most noted of the Jewish writers to witness and to survive the Holocaust: "Man can understand only through words. Jews have never believed in statues, we have never believed in buildings. Judaism is words."[7] And it is by means of words that history—the one subject that Lushinski allows Louisa to read—is created. In their respective attitudes toward "*what really happened*" (Ozick's emphasis) Jew is demarcated from Gentile: Lushinski cares "about the record" while Louisa hates history. In Wiesel's *Night,* one of the most harrowing eyewitness evocations of life in the hell of the Nazi concentration camps, and Raul Hilberg's *The Destruction of the European Jews,* a monumental and exhaustive documentation of Hitler's war against the Jews, Lushinski finds indispensable facts while Louisa senses only the undifferentiated litany of death. Lushinski's passion for Jewish history marks the Jew no less than Louisa's recoil from what she perceives only as senseless morbidity marks the Gentile.

Lushinski, the cosmopolitan mercenary, "the century's one free man," cannot quite wrench himself free from the unwanted embrace of Ziggi, the "black" Jewish child he once was. That effacing one's Jewish identity is futile in any event is shown by the fate of Lushinski's parents who, despite their fair hair, pale eyes, aristocratic manners, and cultivated Polish, are shot for Jews by the Germans. Lushinski and his parents are examples of deracinated Jews who are pressed back into their original Jewish identities despite their best efforts at assimilation. The self-fashioned identities of Lushinski's parents are shattered by the Germans, that of Lushinski by words.

Lushinski's affinity for the words that comprise Holocaust history is not the only vestige of the Jewish identity he so vehemently disclaims. He retains the dark good looks that evoked the childhood nickname Ziggi, "short for *Zigeuner,* the German word for gypsy." The peasants with whom he had been hidden by his parents throw him out, afraid that his "black" features would bring the Nazi Jews-hunters to their door. (The gypsies, for that matter, were also marked for extinction). To be a Jew is to be merely the possessor of a fatal identity that marks its

Bloodshed and Three Novellas

bearer for annihilation. What so diminishes Lushinski is that he yields his Jewish identity not under the irresistible pressure of Nazi persecution but willingly, eagerly, even jokingly when to be a Jew is no longer to be conspicuously at risk. Ironically, it is when he is living most flagrantly the self-fashioned role for which he sacrificed his Jewishness that he is forced back upon his former self. Once on a talk show Lushinski had told about how as a child in the Polish forest he had killed an unidentified man. As he sits "on a blue sofa before an open window" of the white villa on the blue African coast, the setting dissolves into "the bluish snow . . . under the stone-white hanging stars of Poland" (52); and the man Lushinski killed is at last revealed to be Lushinski himself.

"Bloodshed" portrays an ordinary American Jew whose deracination is less a conscious decision à la Lushinski than a drifting into the sort of spiritual malaise that characterizes "successful" assimilation. Bleilip, a nonpracticing lawyer, "a fundraiser by profession" (a deliberate stereotyping, even caricaturing, of the secularized American Jew?), protests too much that he "liked his life, he liked it excessively" (58). Yet the design of Ozick's title story gradually reveals the despair lurking in the heart of a man who feels himself to be not so much a Jew as a "part of society-at-large" (58). A standard tenet of the assimilated (akin to Lushinski's claim not to be part of the Jews but of mankind), Bleilip's self-concept is ironically reductive: wishing to be Everyman, he succeeds only in being no man. This motif of Jews swallowed up by the Gentile culture they try, with varying degrees of success, to ape is, of course, ubiquitous in Ozick's work.

The contrast between Bleilip's pallid Jewishness and that of the Hasidic community he journeys from New

York to visit is immediately apparent. Inhabited mostly by Holocaust survivors or children of survivors, the community strikes Bleilip as "a new town, and everything in it was new or promised" (55). Its newness and rawness, like its several yeshivas, evince a commitment to its many children, to continuity, to the future—in short, to life. Expressed succinctly in the Hebrew toast *L'Chaim* (To Life) is a dedication to the renewal and perpetuation of Jewish communal life. The Hasidic town embodies the survivors' deliberate attempt to reestablish in America a way of life all but obliterated in the European Holocaust. Toby, a distant cousin from an "ordinary" (read "assimilated") family, is regarded by Bleilip as a "convert." Of course the true convert is not Toby, whose life among observant Jews, marriage to the pious Yussel, and bearing of sons approximates the Jewish womanly ideal, but Bleilip, whose deracinated version of Judaism is tantamount to conversion. The contrast, one Ozick never tires of drawing, is not exclusively between Toby and Bleilip but between the Jewish types they represent. Deepening this contrast is the imagery—Yussel's concentration camp tattoo; Bleilip's sense of farness, of seasons displaced, of a foreign bird; an eight-or-nine-year-old snapshot of Toby as she once was but is no longer—of the first several pages of "Bloodshed." A subtle reminder of their differences is couched in Yussel's reaction to Bleilip's offer of the picture: "Why do I need an image? I have my wife right in front of me every morning" (57). That is to say that Yussel possesses the authentic Toby, Bleilip a no-longer-valid semblance. The irrelevance of the photo for Yussel is, moreover, emblematic of the disdain for images imprinted in Jews by the Second Commandment. At the heart of Jewish monotheism lies the concept of a Creator "whose

Covenant summons perpetual self-scrutiny and a continual turning toward moral renewal, and yet *cannot, may not, be physically imagined.*"[8] In their key capitalizations and italicizations Ozick's words define Jewish authenticity even as they set forth the conditions by which authenticity may be attained.

The interplay between the acculturated Bleilip and the orthodox Yussel and Toby spotlights their differences and sets the stage for the more important confrontation between Bleilip and the rebbe (Hasidic mystic) that occupies the greater part of "Bloodshed." Accompanying Yussel to *mincha* (evening prayers), Bleilip strains to understand the rebbe's parable, delivered in a Yiddish-flecked Hebrew, about animal sacrifice in biblical times. The rebbe concludes that after the destruction of the temple and in the absence of Messiah everyone on earth (the Jews first and foremost) became an animal to be sacrificed, most notoriously at the hands of the Nazis. Pointing a finger at Bleilip, the rebbe attributes what he himself has uttered to the visitor's despair, a despair allied with death and opposed to the Jewish *L'Chaim* credo, which upholds the sanctity of life. It may be that Bleilip's despair arises from his inability to reconcile the value of human life with endless Jewish suffering culminating in the Holocaust. Victor Strandberg thus argues that Bleilip's "religious belief fails in the face of recent Jewish history—the bloodshed of the story's title."[9] But this theory rests upon two shaky assumptions: that Bleilip once believed, and that (granted his former belief) his subsequent loss of faith is directly attributable to the Holocaust. Whatever the case, the Bleilip who is exposed by the rebbe has not earned the luxury of despair. Those who have the right to despair, such as the worshiping Hasidim and their rebbe, himself a survivor of Buchenwald, are harshly distinguished from Bleilip. "Who are you?" asks the rebbe, posing the key question of Jewish, not private, identity. "A Jew. Like yourselves. One of you"—Bleilip's instinctive response— is taken by the rebbe for what it is: an unwarranted expression of affiliation. "Presumption," the rebbe calls it; "Atheist, devourer!" he calls Bleilip (67).

Apparently the rebbe's immediate intention is to expose the Jewish pretender, thereby defining Jewish authenticity (as embodied in the Hasidim) in terms of what it is not. Yet the true aim of his diatribe is not permanently to exclude Bleilip from the community of believers but to reveal the means by which the prodigal may be redeemed. To this end the rebbe's denunciation is necessary prologue to the self-awareness, repentance, and spiritual rebirth that constitute the drama of redemption. In the ensuing dialogue the rebbe plays teacher (Bleilip mistakenly, but significantly, addresses him as "rabbi") to Bleilip's pupil who, seated like a child at a school desk, strains to catch phrases of the Yiddish and Hebrew he can barely understand. That Bleilip's comprehension, like that of a child, grows as he listens to the rebbe is evidence of an initiation process at work. And the possibility that an errant Jew can return to the fold is contained in the rebbe's belief in "Turnings. That a man can be turned from folly, error, wrong choices. From misery, evil, private rage. From a mistaken life" (69). Turning is a metaphor for penitential change much favored by Ozick and other Jewish writers. Isaac Bashevis Singer has his protagonist Joseph Shapiro explain the Yiddish title of *The Penitent: "Baal Tschuve* means one who returns. I came back home."[10]

To demonstrate to Bleilip what he reflexively denies— that he has led a "mistaken life"—the rebbe orders him to empty his coat pockets. The two guns that Bleilip successively surrenders—the first a toy, the second real—recall the hitherto unexplained heavy pockets that prompted him to take a taxi in lieu of walking from the bus station to the Hasidic village. It was the presence of these guns, claims Ozick in her preface, that caused her to bury "Bloodshed" in a box for five years. "On account of Chekhov," the Russian master whose influence on twentieth-century fiction and drama is pervasive, her story seemed flawed. Citing Chekhov's dictum that a gun's presence must be established before it goes off, that (in Ozick's phrase) "every surprise must have its subliminal genesis" (6), Ozick regrets the way this advice is turned upside down in "Bloodshed," where a gun is implied, then revealed, but never fired. Like the rebbe in "Bloodshed" who is more afraid of Bleilip's toy gun than the real one, Ozick feared a gun that remained no more than a symbol more than one that could go off. "If I were inventing 'Bloodshed' now," she concludes in her preface, "I would make Bleilip shoot someone; I think I even know whom" (7).

The rebbe accurately reads the guns as tokens of despair despite Bleilip's repeated "I don't have a mistaken life" (72). Tension is generated in "Bloodshed" by playing off this increasingly hollow disclaimer against the many signs of Bleilip's subconscious longing for the meaning and certitude conferred by covenantal Judaism. His reversion to childhood, his vision of his grandfather, his racial memories of Yiddish are all symptoms of turning, for Bleilip has come on pilgrimage to the Hasidic village. That his repressed yearnings for spiritual sustenance draw him closer to authentic Jews is evident in the subtle change in Bleilip's relationship with the rebbe in the concluding paragraphs of "Bloodshed." In the rebbe's confession—that even believers sometimes do not believe—and in Bleilip's halting admission—that even a nonbeliever like himself believes now and then—the two find common ground. After the Holocaust, when the covenant between God and his chosen people seemed frayed, if not rent, even pious Jews like the rebbe grew susceptible to the doubt that afflicts Jews like Bleilip. The inherent kinship among Jews who believe, however much or little, is stated by the rebbe, hard on the heels of Bleilip's confession of belief: "Then you are as bloody as anyone" (72). As in Stephen Crane's American classic *The Red Badge of Courage,* where the blood shed in the Civil War becomes the common denominator binding soldier to soldier, blood, in this case the blood shed by Jews throughout a tragic history culminating in the Holocaust, becomes the red badge of Jewish identity.

"Usurpation (Other People's Stories)" is the most thematically complex of the fictions in *Bloodshed and Three Novellas.* To her overarching concern with Jewish identity and its responsibilities Ozick adds the dilemma of the Jewish artist faced with the conflicting claims of Judaism and art. "Usurpation" is peopled chiefly by writers, all of whom are Jews and each of whom must decide what to write, or whether to write at all. Its strategy is first to demonstrate the essential incompatibility of Judaism and art, then to force a choice between them. This involves an enquiry into the nature of storytelling: its genesis, its material, its ethics. One of Ozick's rare first-person narratives, "Usurpation" is her closest approach to self-referential fiction. As such, the story reflects her own doubts about the creative process and its efficacy for Jews.

And, as usual, "Usurpation" is "the incarnation of an *idea*" (8). Expressed in Ozick's playful but serious reversal of the modernist aesthetic—"Story should not only be but mean"—is the belief that the greater part of a story's value lies in its treatment of ideas. In the preface to *Bloodshed and Three Novellas*—one of her most important critical statements—Ozick clarifies the idea at the heart of "Usurpation," in the process expanding that idea into the basis of a personal literary aesthetic.

Underlying Ozick's uneasiness about the literary enterprise is her belief that English, as a Christian language, may be unacceptable for the transmission of Jewish ideas. Because hers are not "Christian postulates," she finds herself ill served by a medium in which "the oceanic amplitude of the Jewish Idea" cannot be heard. Or perhaps a reader ignorant of or unsympathetic to that idea will be mystified or put off by its fictional incarnation. Whatever the case, the "entire motive" of the preface is to explain "Usurpation," which was judged incomprehensible by Anatole Broyard, "an intelligent reviewer."

> "Usurpation" is a story written against story-writing; against the Muse-goddesses; against Apollo. It is against magic and mystification, against show and "miracle," and, going deeper into the dark, against idolatry. It is an invention directed against inventing— the point being that the story-making faculty itself can be a corridor to the corruptions and abominations of idol-worship, of the adoration of magical event (11).

Unable to write in a Jewish language in which the story "would have been understood instantly," Ozick, like the several writers in "Usurpation," must choose among three alternatives, all unappealing: to express the "Jewish Idea," however opaquely; to express ideas alien to Judaism; or to cease writing altogether. Driven to write but in dread of the imagination, the writer who would remain Jewish must prefer, however reluctantly, the first alternative.

"Usurpation" rests on the assumption that its writers, even those who, like Ozick herself, "dread the cannibal touch of story-making," nevertheless, again like Ozick, "lust after stories more and more and more" (12). In their rage to write they appropriate "Other People's Stories," emulating the cannibalism of "Usurpation" itself: Ozick's magic crown of silver that confers literary fame on its wearer owes its genesis to Bernard Malamud's "The Silver Crown" (in *Rembrandt's Hat*). The female writer who narrates "Usurpation" attends a reading by a famous author at which she is overcome with lust for his story of a magical silver crown. Ozick herself was present at the 92nd Street Y when "The Silver Crown" was read; in "Usurpation" the reader's appearance, notably his "whitening mustache," matches Malamud's. Alex (the "goat") lives and writes in an abandoned tenement about to be torn down; he "stole the idea from a book" (160), transparently Malamud's *The Tenants*, a novel reviewed by Ozick. The "old writer of Jerusalem" destined to win the Nobel Prize is S. Y. Agnon; his portrayal is inspired by David Stern's "Agnon: A Story." Readers familiar with Agnon recognize him as the author of the short fable about why the Messiah tarries, which the ghost of Tchernikhovsky so much admires in "Usurpation." Tchernikhovsky, a famous Jewish poet, is also employed by Ozick. His ghost utters the word "expired," which ends the narrator's reworking (more usurpation) of the goat's

Bloodshed and Three Novellas

"A Story of Youth and Homage" and echoes the last word of Malamud's "The Silver Crown" (still another usurpation). It is, moreover, from Tchernikhovsky's "Before the Statue of Apollo" that Ozick lifts the striking metaphor of the whips which like phylacteries (two small square leather boxes containing slips inscribed with scriptural passages, one worn on the left arm, the other on the forehead of Jewish men at prayer) bind the forehead and arms of the narrator at the end of "Usurpation."

"Usurpation" is shaped by its many borrowings. Its frame tale begins with the narrator's account of "her" story, usurped by the famous writer and read by him at the 92nd Street Y before she could write it out. This tale of a phony rabbi who sold silver crowns, found by the famous writer in a newspaper, is itself a usurpation. At the reading the goat presses his manuscript—"A Story of Youth and Homage"—on the reluctant narrator. Not only its title but its plot—an ambitious young writer lusts after the enviable reputation of an older one—suggests usurpation. Soon after the moment in the manuscript when the old writer (Agnon) advises his would-be successor to adopt the ways of the *ba'al ga'avah* (the supplanter who conceals his audacity by feigning shyness), the narrator breaks off her retelling of what was the goat's tale but is henceforth her own. What follows is a fiction born of the forced marriage between the goat's story and Malamud's: "Stealing from two disparate tales I smashed their elements one into the other" (157).

Ozick uses crowns to unify these "disparate tales." A symbol of the false or idolatrous values attained by the ambitious writers who successively wear it, the crown retains deceptive properties carried over from the 92nd Street Y reading. Writers who lust after the silver crown of literary fame reveal their moral shortcomings in "Usurpation." Of dubious value and indeterminate power, a device to elicit truth in "The Silver Crown," the magic crown becomes a far less neutral symbol in "Usurpation." Ozick employs it as a malevolent force tempting writers to violate Jewish law in pursuit of the fame and immortality associated with pagan idolatry. Only the old writer (Agnon), who properly refuses to remove the crown from its box, proves impervious to its blandishments. And it is he who ironically achieves the undying fame so fervently desired by the other writers. Agnon voices the credo of "Usurpation": "All that is not law is levity" (147, 177). He "threads his tales with strands of the holy phrases" (140), in contrast to the narrator, who would "throw over being a Jew," and Tchernikhovsky, who pursued the "old gods of Canaan" (144). Because Agnon eschews "the occult darknesses of random aesthetics" for the "illuminations of liturgy," his stories will endure while those of Jewish writers who give themselves "over altogether to Gentile culture" will "be lost to history."[11]

To amplify the evil associated with the crown Ozick expands it from a nascent symbol of an aesthetic forbidden to Jews into an active scourge for those apostates who nonetheless put it on. The siren song of fame proves equally seductive for the narrator. Although she has filched the crown for her own story, endowing it in the process with the fatal powers that destroy the goat's ambitious student, she herself also falls victim to its "magic." That she feels the weight of the crown pressing "unerringly into the secret tunnels of my brain," its every point "a spear, a nail" (176), invokes the dilemma of the modern Jewish writer seemingly forced to choose between faith and art. When the narrator opts for art, choosing

Apollo over the Name of Names, a flood of stories, all of them usurped, streams from her. Only the phylacteries save her from the fate suffered by the ambitious student, binding her again to the Jewish covenant she had forsaken. Perhaps her apostasy was more apparent than real, the gushing stories a fleeting wish-fulfillment. Or perhaps the narrator is saved because "Usurpation" is, after all, her story, to end in whatever manner she deems fit.

Whatever the case, the story functions as literary criticism, arguing powerfully for centrally liturgical Jewish writing and against the magic, demonic, pantheistic, ultimately pagan writing of Tchernikhovsky. That the "Canaanite idols" worshiped by Tchernikhovsky end by calling him "kike" illustrates the wages of idolatry. Since, according to the Agnon of "Usurpation," without Torah (law) the Jewish writer is capable only of levity; and since, according to Ozick, a non-Jewish language cannot express the "Jewish Idea" (thus her explanatory preface), it would appear that a covenantal literature written exclusively in Hebrew or Yiddish should be the sole aim of the Jewish writer. The real Agnon once proposed that, since only the "Holy Tongue" guarantees literary survival, the Jewish writer could only be "safe" by seeing to it that his works were translated into Hebrew.[12] Yet this "solution" is at best a compromise for those, Ozick included, who write in one of the languages of "exile." Like the narrator of "Usurpation"—which is "above all" about "the dread of idols; the dread of the magic that kills. The dread of imagination"—Ozick is condemned endlessly to "dread the cannibal touch of story-making" even as she lusts more and more after stories.

As a cautionary tale "Usurpation" dramatizes the fear of fiction that must affect any writer who wishes to remain wholly Jewish. Although Agnon's stories, threaded "with strands of the holy phrases," are invoked as examples of permissible (i.e., liturgical) writing, "Usurpation" achieves its purpose by citing the vastly more prevalent subject matter that, in the "terrible Hebrew word," is *asur* (forbidden). Because storytelling smacks of the "magic" of pagan myth and Christian Eucharist, nearly all fiction is suspect. The "safest" topics—those which may legitimately confer a silver crown—are necessarily rooted, if not specifically in Torah, then at least broadly in the truths of the Jewish experience. Chief among these truths in the modern era is the Holocaust, the historical moment which tests Jewish identity whether in the macabre sense of being earmarked for extermination or simply of acknowledging the bond (like the phylacteries that wind about the narrator's arms) that binds together all Jews, selected and spared alike. "Usurpation" is no exception to the rule that Ozick's stories invariably contain references, however subliminal, to the Holocaust. Thus the Brooklyn street visited by the narrator in search of the goat "was a place where there had been conflagrations" (159). Although Herzl Street (named after the Zionist founder of modern Israel) was once a Jewish enclave, no Jews remain in the "burned out" buildings. The narrator and the goat take turns reading Saul's papers (ostensible source of "The Magic Crown") which deal with the relationship between God and Jews. Their reading culminates in a typical story of Holocaust victims who are not saved by God's miraculous intervention. The moral of the story—"if you talk miracle, that's where everything becomes false" (171)—is a thinly veiled warning against the fictionalizing process. Denying "sorcery," sneering at "magic," deriding "de-

mons,'' Saul professes those Jewish ideas which are antithetical to the ''forbidden'' storytelling that attracts the
narrator. The unsought crowns worn by Saul, his wife,
and the goat symbolize their fidelity to the facts of Jewish
experience. Their crowning strongly implies the superiority of Saul's crudely written fragments about Jews to the
polished Apollonian verses of Tchernikhovsky and to the
equally pagan stories the narrator dreams of writing.

The Shawl

Holocaust imagery—just perceptible in ''An Education,'' unmissable in ''A Mercenary'' and ''Usurpation,''
essential in ''Bloodshed''—is a key component of liturgical consciousness in the fictions that comprise *Bloodshed
and Three Novellas*. Since, however, nearly all of Ozick's
settings are American and contemporary, the Holocaust,
no matter how poignantly invoked, is inevitably distanced
by space and time. While the Holocaust must retain its
centrality for contemporary American Jews, the majority
of Ozick's fictional characters have no direct experience
of the bloodshed of the title. Only in *The Shawl* (1989)
does Ozick treat the Nazi death camps in the full horror of
their immediacy.[13] Fittingly, its genesis is historical, inspired by a single line in William Shirer's massive *The
Rise and Fall of the Third Reich* ''that spoke about babies
being thrown against the electrified fences.''[14] To confront
such material head on proved excruciatingly difficult for
Ozick. If storytelling is itself a risky business—the lesson
of ''Usurpation''—how much riskier must it be to make
art out of the Holocaust. ''I worry very much,'' said
Ozick, ''that this subject is corrupted by fiction and that

fiction in general corrupts history.''[15] Like many postwar Jewish writers Ozick is torn between the fear of trivializing the Holocaust and the belief in the necessity of bearing witness to its enormities.

Those enormities are crystallized in "The Shawl" when a German guard hurls Magda, Rosa's starving baby, onto the electrified fence of the concentration camp. That the story's forced marches, numbing cold, constant hunger, excremental stench, random brutality, and innocent victims seem all too familiar testifies to the success of Jewish writers in preserving the Holocaust in the collective memory. In the story's few pages cluster together the atrocities that will sear Rosa's memory in the far longer sequel to "The Shawl." Like that of so many death camp survivors, Rosa's future identity will be fatally determined by what she has witnessed and endured "in a place without pity." Most remarkable in the story, however, is the shawl itself—a symbol of life amidst the many symbols of death. Wrapped in the shawl, baby Magda "milked" its corner, relinquishing Rosa's dry teats uncomplainingly. A "magic shawl, it could nourish an infant for three days and three nights"; without it Magda "should have been dead already" (5). When Stella, Rosa's fourteen-year-old niece, desperately cold, took the shawl away, she "made Magda die." Grieving for the loss of her shawl, the normally silent Magda utters her first cry, thereby fatally attracting a guard's attention. Too late, Rosa snatches the shawl from Stella: Magda is already hurtling through the air in the direction of the electrified fence. Only by stuffing the shawl into her own mouth to stifle the "wolf's screech" involuntarily rising in her throat does Rosa save herself. Drinking the shawl in unconscious imitation of her lost daughter, Rosa tastes the same "cinnamon and almond depth of Magda's saliva'' (10), all that remains of the murdered child.

Successively nourishing Magda, warming Stella, and saving Rosa, the magic shawl is a life preserver in a sea of death. A general symbol of life, the shawl nonetheless has specifically Jewish bearings. It unites its three wearers in a mini-community of sufferers, a microcosm of the persecuted Jewish millions. As the whips that curl around the narrator of "Usurpation" become phylacteries that bind her to her fellow Jews, so the shawl becomes an equally potent symbol of Jewish affiliation—the tallit, or Jewish prayer shawl. Like phylacteries, the tallit is a ritual object donned at prayer when Jews, in no small part because they wear the common talismans of their faith, draw closer to their God and become most fully members of the covenant community. A more obscure but equally valid aspect of the shawl's symbolism may be suggested by its distinctive smell and taste:

> The peculiar aroma of cinnamon and almonds, itself so out of place in the midst of death, corpses, and wind bearing the black ash from crematoria, evokes a quasimystical image of the *besamin* (spice) box. Jews sniff the *besamin* at the *havadalah* ceremony which marks the outgoing of the Sabbath, thereby sustaining themselves for the rigors and tribulations of the profane or ordinary days of the week. By utilizing the prayer shawl and spice box imagery, and paranormal phenomena usually associated with the mystical element of Judaism, Ozick's tale conveys the message that the bleakness of the historical moment is not the final chapter in Jewish existence. Jewish religious creativity and covenantal symbolism can occur even under the

most extreme conditions. The eternality of Israel is symbolized when Rosa and Stella survive the death camps and come to America.[16]

In America some thirty years later the eponymous heroine of "Rosa," now "a madwoman and a scavenger," has exchanged one form of living death for another. Miami—where the "streets were a furnace, the sun an executioner"—is for Rosa an updated version of a concentration camp. "Where I put myself is in hell' (14), she writes to Stella in New York. Having survived the worst, Rosa has come to regard it as a permanent condition. Stella is the "Angel of Death," the old Jews transplanted from New York to Florida "all scarecrows, blown about under the murdering sunball with empty ribcages" (16). Like so many of the Holocaust survivors who inhabit postwar Jewish literature, Rosa considers herself no longer truly alive. Symptomatic of Rosa's hopelessness is the reduction of the shawl from Jewish emblem to a personal fetish. Clinging to the shawl, Rosa calls back her murdered daughter and aborted past. In so doing, however, she invokes a scenario that, for all its "real" life, is emblematic of death.

Escape and denial converge in the two letters Rosa writes to the long-dead Magda, letters which reinvent the past even as they invoke it. Addressed to a Magda successively imagined as a beautiful young woman of thirty-one, a doctor married to a doctor and living in a "large house in Mamaroneck, NY" (35); a professor of Greek philosophy at Columbia University in New York City" (39); and a girl of sixteen, "all in flower" (64), the letters ironically transform Rosa's evasions into modes of thematic clarification. That Rosa writes in "the most excellent literary Polish'' (14) to Magda but in crude English to Stella—who has forgotten their mother tongue—is itself significant. By deliberately refusing to learn English, Rosa lives in the pre-Holocaust Polish past; by abandoning Polish for English, Stella lives in the post-Holocaust American present. Yet Rosa's retreat into a past sanitized and idealized in her imagination is more to be pitied than condemned. What diminishes Rosa is not that she forges through language a link with the past but rather that her elegant Polish disavows her Jewish heritage—in Miami as it did in Warsaw. The first letter to Magda recalls Rosa's father—a ''Pole by right''—and mother who ''wanted so much to convert'' and who, ''attracted'' to Catholicism, ''let the maid keep a statue of the Virgin and Child in the kitchen'' (41). The second letter further distances Rosa and her family from their fellow Jews—''peasants worn out from their rituals and superstitions, phylacteries on their foreheads sticking up so stupidly'' (67). Symbolically opposed to these holy emblems of Jewish affiliation—ridiculed by Rosa as ''unicorn's horns''—are the replicas of Greek vases and the modern ink drawings which filled her parents' house. This juxtaposition of the Jewish holy and the Gentile profane recalls the similar opposition of phylacteries to pagan verse in ''Usurpation.'' But it is their preference for Polish—the language of the Gentiles—and their contempt for Yiddish—the language of the Jews—that chiefly effected the willful separation of Rosa's family from their coreligionists. Wholly acculturated Jews who belonged to the Polish society into which they were born, Rosa and her family—like their thoroughly assimilated German counterparts—were incredulous when their ''patrimony'' was brutally stripped from them by the Nazis. Hitler's war against the Jews made no distinction between the pious and the profane. No matter that Rosa cries out: "I'm not like those other Jews"; in the relentless grip of their persecutors all Jews attained a terrible equality. And all the murdered Jews, including those universalists who, like Rosa, denied their Jewish heritage, "rend our heart, our sense of mercy and of justice," says Ozick. "But I think the Jews who went to their deaths not knowing why, but knowing the meaning of their lives as Jews, were in some sense more redeemed in the eyes of history than those who went with a sense of mistaken identity."[17]

Rosa's type of prewar Jew—highly assimilated, extremely cultivated—was inspired by Jerzy Kosinski. Speaking of the richness of the Polish language and of its Jewish adherents, Kosinski reminded Ozick that not all East European Jews fit the *shtetl* stereotype.[18] In prewar Warsaw, Rosa and her family idolized Gentile culture; in postwar America, Rosa preserves vestiges of that culture only in the elegant Polish of her pathetic letters to Magda. And it is the lost Magda who becomes for Rosa an object of veneration. Magda is a saint, the shawl she once was wrapped in a holy relic. Stella accuses Rosa of being "like those people in the Middle Ages who worshipped a piece of the True Cross" (31–32). Still, the worship of Magda is no isolated phenomenon but simply the most overt manifestation of Rosa's habit of idolizing the past. To idolize is to idealize: Rosa selectively alters the past in much the same way that she converts a dead baby into a living "Queen of Bloom and Blossom" (66). Idealization becomes, in turn, a mode of evasion, a strategy for living in and sealing off a past scraped free of Nazi murderers. To obliterate the fact of her own rape by a German and the consequent birth of Magda, whose blue eyes and yellow hair give her the appearance of "one of *their* babies," Rosa invents for Magda a father named Andrzej. The son of a converted Jew married to a Gentile, his conspicuously Polish name betrays Rosa's typical rejection of all that is Jewish as well as her understandable need to conceal the truth of Magda's parentage.

Psychologically encapsulated in the past, Rosa cannot be dragged into the present by Stella, whose unvarnished memories of the Holocaust are dismissed as "pornography." Only in the attentions—initially spurned—of Persky, like herself a former resident of Warsaw, does the possibility exist that Rosa can be cajoled—or jolted—into renewed life. But Persky, who left Warsaw in 1920, can no more share Rosa's past than can the "bloodsucker" clinical psychologist Dr. Tree, who plagues her with requests to take part in his studies of concentration camp survivors. Rosa's repeated "My Warsaw isn't your Warsaw" draws a valid distinction between refugees like Persky and survivors like herself. More invidious is her snobbish identification with the Warsaw of the Gentiles and her antipathy toward the rotting ghetto of the Jews. Persky's attempt to speak with her in Yiddish conjures up memories of how her parents "mocked at" the language of the Jews. Ignorance of Yiddish—the common language of European Jews—is for Rosa only a positive indicator of social status. In the context of *The Shawl,* however, Rosa's contempt for Yiddish reflects her general rejection of Jewishness. Persky's attempts to restore her to life arise from his instinctive sense of their mutual affiliation. To the extent that Rosa denies Jewish mutuality, she would seem to be restoration-proof.

The novella retains its tension between death and rebirth until the end. When Rosa opens Stella's package, the shawl seems to lie inertly in its box, drained of its customary power to restore Magda instantly. Yet shortly thereafter, speaking long distance to Stella, Rosa covers the receiver with the shawl, and the "whole room was full of Magda" (64). Only in the novella's last several paragraphs, after Magda's shade begins turning away, do Rosa's actions suggest rebirth. The clamor of the shawled telephone, "so long comatose—now . . . ardent with its cry" (70), dispels the dead Magda as it announces the living Persky. Agreeing to see Persky, Rosa takes the shawl from the phone: "Magda was away." To welcome Persky is to admit the possibility of post-Holocaust life. Because he so patently represents the type of Jew reviled by her family in prewar Warsaw, to see Persky is also to acknowledge her own Jewish identity and her solidarity not only with the Jewish dead but with the Jewish living. This is not to say that Rosa's reentry into the world of the living is contingent upon forgetting Magda and discarding the shawl. An eyewitness to history's greatest infamy, Rosa must continue to honor the memory of the sacred dead, not by worshiping them but by preserving the Holocaust in the collective memory.

NOTES

1. Ozick, *Bloodshed and Three Novellas* (New York: Knopf, 1976). Page references in parentheses are to this edition.

2. Victor Strandberg, "The Art of Cynthia Ozick," *Texas Studies in Literature and Language* 25 (Summer 1983) 301–02.

3. Ozick, *Art and Ardor* (New York: Knopf, 1983) 294.

4. Ozick, *Metaphor and Memory* (New York: Knopf, 1989) 58.

5. Catherine Rainwater and William J. Scheick, "An Interview with Cynthia Ozick, (Summer 1982)," *Texas Studies in Literature and Language* 25 (Summer 1983) 257.

6. *Art and Ardor* 177. The shofar, a ram's horn blown at the New Year, symbolically recalls the ram that was sacrificed in place of Isaac.

7. Lily Edelman, "A Conversation with Elie Wiesel," *Responses to Elie Wiesel*, ed. H. J. Cargas (New York: Person Books, 1978) 21.

8. *Metaphor and Memory* 253.

9. Strandberg 305.

10. Isaac Bashevis Singer, *The Penitent* (New York: Farrar, Straus, 1983) 5.

11. *Art and Ardor* 177.

12. Ozick, *Metaphor and Memory* 211.

13. Ozick, *The Shawl* (New York: Knopf, 1989). Page references in parentheses are to this edition.

14. Francine Prose, "Idolatry in Miami," *The New York Times Book Review* 10 Sept. 1989: 39.

15. Prose 39.

16. Alan L. Berger, *Crisis and Covenant: The Holocaust in American Jewish Fiction* (Albany: State University of New York Press, 1985) 54.

17. Richard Bernstein, "On Being Nice or Rotten in Writing," *The New York Times* 3 Oct. 1989: 14.

18. Bernstein 14.

CHAPTER FIVE

Levitation: Five Fictions

Fantasy, an aspect of Ozick's writing strategy in *The Pagan Rabbi* and *Bloodshed,* is the shaping force in *Levitation: Five Fictions.* Characters dream, and in dreaming release the fantasies which in turn give the stories their form and meaning. Whatever their primary theme—Jewish identity in the title story; artistic creation in ''Shots''; or Jewishness and creativity allied to feminism in the story and novella featuring Ruth Puttermesser which together make up more than half of *Levitation*'s pages—the stories are grounded in the convergence of reality and fantasy. Invariably reality is thereby conditioned, subverted, or absorbed by fantasy. What characteristically emerges is a new reality, as in Shakespeare's festive comedies such as *A Midsummer Night's Dream* which employ fantasy as a means of clarification.

''Levitation'' begins as a comic satire on a type of postmodern writing in general and on the novel-writing Feingolds in particular. As a New York Jewish writer writing about writers writing, Ozick may be poking fun at the self-referential fiction so prevalent in the 1960s and 1970s, and at herself for ostensibly following a moribund fashion. That several of Ozick's most powerful stories, including "Envy" and "Usurpation," are about writers and writing contributes to the slyly self-deprecating opening of "Levitation." Although sporadically tempted to write about New York writers, the Feingolds disdain such writing, which they refer to as "Forbidden City." Blissfully unaware of anxieties about the exhaustion of forms and even about the death of the novel that engendered self-referential fiction, the Feingolds dedicate themselves to the traditional literary values of pictorial accuracy and psychological realism. Of course the fact that all this creative earnestness has resulted in only one published novel apiece and that the Feingolds are self-confessed "secondary people" adds dimension to the literary satire. As ineffectual apologists for literary realism the Feingolds reflect its sometime inadequacies and lend credence to Ozick's own method of leavening reality with fantasy. The Feingolds are also skewered as representatives of a sub-species of New York literati. Because everything about them—his editorial job, her publisher, their books—is as relentlessly "secondary-level" as themselves, the Feingolds plan a cocktail party to which they invite Irving Howe, Susan Sontag, Alfred Kazin, all high-powered intellectuals, like Ozick herself. None of the luminaries comes, and the Feingolds' apartment fills up with people much like themselves.

The failure of the cocktail party ("No one's here," Feingold repeats) and the attendant failure of the Feingolds to transcend, however briefly, their "secondary-level" status, might provide a nice ending to a literary satire. Instead the failed cocktail party becomes the setting for the real drama of "Levitation" as the story veers into an entirely new direction adumbrated only faintly in its beginning. From the opening paragraphs to the onset of the cocktail party, the Feingolds are treated as a pair, their singular identities subsumed in a mutual outlook. But the first page of the story also makes clear the central fact of their marriage: that Feingold and Lucy, coming from antithetical traditions, are drawn together chiefly by his wish for a Gentile wife, hers for a "Hebrew" husband. Despite her conversion to Judaism and her disavowal of her legacy as a minister's daughter, it is the ultimate chasm between husband and wife that is revealed in the byplay of the cocktail party. Two devices signal the story's inevitable shift from mutuality to separation. Lucy's point of view, hitherto identical to Feingold's, detaches itself from his to become the central consciousness of the story. And the party guests are likewise separated, the Jews congregating in the living room, the Gentiles and the sort of Jews "who went off to studio showings of *Screw on Screen* on the eve of the Day of Atonement"[1] in the dining room. It is in the living room, then, that Feingold has what Lucy calls "one of his spasms of fanaticism," compulsively recounting the medieval anti-Semitic atrocities that are the subject of his work in progress. The growing intensity of Feingold's diatribe and of the felt Jewishness in the living room effect the explicit cleaving of what remains of the couple's united identity. This "terrible intensity" of the Jews, rising to fever pitch when a refugee updates Feingold's catalog of ancient persecution with the modern horrors of the Holocaust which he has witnessed, strikes Lucy as all but inexplicable: "*They* were intense all the time; . . . was it because they had been Chosen?" (14). Ozick's italicization of *They* and capitalization of Chosen spotlight Lucy's reflexive awareness of the chasm that, despite her conversion, exists between the Jews in the living room and herself. Indeed, she can envision Jewish suffering only in Christian terms, the refugee's Holocaust images invoking not charred corpses but multitudes of Crucifixions: "Every Jew was Jesus."

Lucy's reversion to Christianity is the necessary prelude—the minor epiphany—to her fantasy of the rising room—the major epiphany—that fills the last several pages of "Levitation." "It portrays the Holocaust as an identity-defining device, levitating genuine Jews away from pseudo or de-Judaized Jews who remain below on ground level."[2] Like the shift to Lucy's point of view and her instinctive recourse to Christian imagery, the ascending room is therefore a means of defining Jewishness by showing what a Jew is not. Alone at the bottom of the room, Lucy can only be taken by, can only listen to, Jesus. Unable, or unwilling, to share with the levitating Jews the definitive modern Jewish experience—the Holocaust—Lucy becomes the receptacle of attitudes and images that for Ozick characterize the non-Jew. Within the ambit of the levitating room Lucy imagines herself and her children in a city park (significantly, Feingold is absent, napping at home) surrounded by a motley crowd of musicians and dancers, all celebrating nature. It is no accident that Lucy's ecstatic vision of nature worship "sees what is eternal": the Christian Madonna as the apotheosis of successive fertility goddesses—Astarte, Aphrodite, Venus. This equation of pagan rites with all that is non-Jewish is, of course, a restatement of a familiar Ozick theme. Its corollary is found in the Jewish distrust of nature as an irrational force and nature worship as antithetical to Jewish monotheism and threatening to Jewish existence. For Ozick it is a form of idolatry, a violation of the Second Commandment with its litmus test of religious

Understanding Cynthia Ozick

identity. Announced initially in *Trust* as the Pan versus Moses theme, this conflict between forms of worship and ultimately of belief systems has already animated such powerful Ozick fictions as "The Pagan Rabbi" and "Usurpation (Other People's Stories)." While the theme is ubiquitous in Ozick's work, it is by no means absent in that of other Jewish writers. Especially in twentieth-century Jewish literature nature worship has come to be identified with those atavistic impulses that culminated in the Holocaust.

That the Jews are a chosen people—only they need resist the siren song of nature and its attendant worship and hew steadfastly to the Second Commandment—is explicit in "Levitation." Floating in air, the authentic Jews in the Feingolds' living room are united not only by the ultimate tragedy—the Holocaust—but by the idea of covenant. At that moment when, according to the orthodox, *all* Jews— past, present, and future—stood together on Sinai and a unique relationship was forged by God with His chosen people, Jewish identity was forever stamped. Thenceforth it is the differences, not the similarities, between "them" and "us" that are most remarkable. The last paragraphs of "Levitation" find Lucy taking refuge from her airborne Jewish guests in the dining room, where she is relieved to hear the talk of "atheists." In this final separation—Lucy from Feingold, idolater from monotheist, Gentile from Jew—lies the meaning of "Levitation."

In varying degrees the remaining stories in *Levitation: Five Fictions* take up subject and methodology established in the title story. All are concerned with identity, feminine as well as Jewish; and all depend upon fantasies often as extravagant as Lucy's vision of soaring Jews in "Levitation." Two fictions, together comprising more than half

the volume, feature Ruth Puttermesser, a New York Jewish intellectual and "something of a feminist," like Ozick
herself. And like Ozick ("I am nicer in life than I am in
my writing")[3] Puttermesser—the name translates as But-
terknife—combines emotional warmth with hard intelligence. Puttermesser—only her mother and her lover call
her Ruth—also shares with Ozick an intense Jewishness
and a voracious appetite for all sorts of literature. A recurring fantasy finds Puttermesser in her own version of
Eden where gorging herself on fudge risks no tooth decay
and where she "will read Non-Fiction into eternity; and
there is still time for Fiction" (33). Although she dreams
a paradise of books and candy, Puttermesser, an urbanite
and a lawyer, is no escapist. Above all, she is committed—to ideas, to the law, to her Jewish heritage, and to
New York, city of her birth and her lifelong home.
"Puttermesser: Her Work History, Her Ancestry, Her Afterlife," the first and shorter of the two Puttermesser stories, functions as selective, compressed, occasionally
parodic biography. Here the biographer-narrator examines
Puttermesser not "as an artifact but as an essence." The
narrative corresponds to the first two divisions—"Her
Work History" and "Her Ancestry"—of its title. "Her
Afterlife" consists of part of a dream sequence and of
scattered authorial revelations about her future. Her later
life belongs more properly to "Puttermesser and Xanthippe," a novella whose lengthier form reflects Puttermesser's expanding role in the public world.

But it is Puttermesser's private world that is most often
invoked to capture her "essence" in the first story. Beginning with a realistic though abbreviated chronology of the
life of Puttermesser, a lawyer of thirty-four when the story
opens, the narrative dissolves into an ever more revealing

psychic biography arising from her dreams. Details of her life invariably evidence the intensity of her attachments—to the "same endlessly mazy apartment she had grown up in" (21); to her adolescent studies and piano lessons (aging music sheets marked by her teacher still atop the upright piano); to her profession of law; above all to her Jewish past and its perpetuation. Thus she clings to her parents' apartment in the decaying Bronx (they had moved to Miami Beach), roaming in the "furry slippers left over from high school" through the same rooms in which she had spent her youth. While her living arrangements may reflect as much her disdain for the typical New York cubbyhole of an apartment as her sentimental clinging to the world of her parents, they also signify an ongoing commitment to the Jewish past which the old apartment and neighborhood represent. Puttermesser's Jewishness, most obvious in her looks ("one of those Jewish faces with a vaguely Oriental cast"), is less obvious in her choice of professions. Yet the law, for Puttermesser, is no ticket to prosperity or prestige; rather it is the logical and ethical locus of her Jewish reverence for the word, otherwise manifest in her studiousness and omnivorous reading. Implicit in her quitting her first job with a tony law firm for an ostensibly unrewarding career in municipal administration is her concept of law not as a guarantor of corporate profits but as a vehicle of social justice. That the former job was uncongenial to Puttermesser both as woman and Jew (she sees her hiring by the "blueblood Wall Street firm" as double tokenism) effects the same separation of "us" from "them" that marks "Levitation." The partners' Jewish quotas (three Jews are hired, a different three leave, each year), their easy assumption of their own superiority ("divine right"), and

Levitation: Five Fictions

their bland refusal to understand anyone different from themselves announce the familiar Ozick theme of Jewish uniqueness. Thus the firm's young male Jews seem outwardly indistinguishable from their colleagues, yet "the athletic clubs would not have them" (25).

Leaving the firm of Midland, Reid & Cockleberry is no automatic assertion of Puttermesser's Jewish identity. Far more significant is her study of Hebrew grammar, which Puttermesser sees "as a code for the world's design, indissoluble, predetermined, translucent" (24). It is this crucial idea of language as a way of seeing, and of the Hebrew language as indispensable to the Jewish way of seeing, that recurs so often in Ozick's work, fiction and nonfiction alike. In her essay "The Fourth Sparrow: The Magisterial Reach of Gershom Scholem," for example, Ozick pays tribute to the famous Jewish historian "who has remade the world." But in order to pursue the cosmos, Scholem had to delve beyond the Greek and Roman underpinnings of his classical European education, back "to the perplexities of Genesis and the Hebrew language."[4] Puttermesser's resemblance to her creator is nowhere more apparent than in her hard striving to master Hebrew and with it the key to a uniquely Jewish world view. An offshoot of Ozick's oft-stated belief that the various languages of the Diaspora cannot help but reflect values historically opposed and often inimical to Judaism, the learning of Hebrew becomes in her fiction a powerful assertion of Jewish identity. Puttermesser's unabashed Jewishness is counterpointed by Ozick's reminder that Dreyfus, a perfect Frenchman who spoke perfect French, was the same type as the officers who condemned him. Commissioner Guggenheim at the Municipal Building, a German Jew who cultivates rich Gentiles "who let him eat with them but warned their daughters against him'' (30), no less than the male Jews who assiduously ape their fellow lawyers at Midland, Reid & Cockleberry yet are barred from athletic clubs, is a comic caricature of an assimilated Jew.

Puttermesser's Jewish identity in all its richness is most fully expressed in the reverie that comprises the story's second half. This ''luxuriant dream'' (''Her Afterlife'') of a ''reconstituted Garden of Eden'' where the insatiable Puttermesser will forever gorge herself on fudge and literature preludes a return to the apparent reality of twice-weekly Hebrew lessons with Uncle Zindel (''Her Ancestry''). Only a couple of pages later is it revealed that Puttermesser's relationship with Zindel is no less a dream than her sojourn in Eden, and that the story contains a hitherto unsuspected narrative layer. An intruding voice tells Puttermesser's biographer to stop the narrative, to desist from treating the Zindel episode as true when the truth is that the uncle died four years before Puttermesser's birth. In another sort of fiction the voice that stops the freely inventing biographer might be an aspect of the literary gamesmanship played by the self-reflexive author, the ''real'' narrator. But Ozick, as usual, is more interested in the complexities of Jewish identity than in those of narrative structure. So deep-seated, even desperate, is Puttermesser's need for a viable Jewish past that her biographer conspires with her to ''claim an ancestor.'' Refusing to identify the Zindel episode as a dream, refusing in other words to tell the ''truth,'' the biographer ironically achieves biography's ultimate goal: the fullest possible revelation of its subject. Infusing the literal data of Puttermesser's quotidian life with the stuff of her dreams, the biographer captures the essential Puttermesser. Although

it is the biographer's egregious expansion of a Puttermesser–Zindel relationship that could never have existed
that outrages the supernarrator—"A symbol is allowed,
but not a whole scene: do not accommodate too obsequi-
ously to Puttermesser's romance"(35)—it is most precisely in those imagined moments with Uncle Zindel that
Puttermesser is most fully herself.

Puttermesser's dream of Uncle Zindel is triggered by
her yearning for "connection—surely a Jew must own a
past" (36). She clings to a Zindel who died four years
before her birth as a surrogate for the Jewish ancestry she
so conspicuously lacks. Daughter of Americanized parents, brought up in a world without a past, Puttermesser
invents Uncle Zindel as a means of reinventing herself.
Twice a week she imagines herself taking Hebrew lessons
from Zindel, former *shammes* (sexton) of a *shul* (synagogue), observer of the Sabbath, eater of kosher meat—
everything her father was not. That Puttermesser falls
"into so poignant a fever over the cracked phrases of a
shammes of a torn-down shul" (36) strikes the intruding
narrator as inexplicable. Yet in this scrupulously truthful
narrator's disclosure that the shul was not even torn down
but had simply disintegrated, its aging congregation—and
shammes—flaking away, lies the explanation for Puttermesser's obsessive restructuring of a past that never was.
For the crumbled shul and scattered worshipers are symbolic of the dissolution of the Jewish community. And
while Puttermesser cannot halt the corrosion in contemporary America of Jewish belief, she can at least arrest it in
herself. Clinging to Uncle Zindel, Puttermesser delves beyond the blandness of her own "real" ancestry and of
Jewish life in America back to the flat-roofed house in the
little town—no less redolent of the Jewish past for being

apocryphal—of his birth. Puttermesser, "loyal to certain environments," senses destiny in geography: Jews have successively disappeared from Zindel's European birthplace, from their first American "home" on New York's lower East Side, even from the Bronx where Puttermesser herself survives as a Jewish anachronism among blacks and Hispanics. Aged Jews such as Puttermesser's parents cluster together in Miami Beach, their final habitat and resting place. With their deaths the Jewish past will recede even further beyond Puttermesser's straining eyes, to be visible only in scraps of newspaper and fading photographs. Like Holocaust survivors and Ozick herself, Puttermesser is haunted by the specter of Jewish extinction. No wonder that she is driven by the pathetic, yet heroic, need to recover a language, a geography, a past, a people—if only in the world of dreams.

"Hey! Puttermesser's biographer! What will you do with her now?" "Puttermesser and Xanthippe," the novella that concludes *Levitation: Five Fictions* and takes up half its pages, answers this question posed by the supernarrator at the end of "Puttermesser: Her Work History, Her Ancestry, Her Afterlife." The first of the novella's twelve episodes is as realistic as the opening pages of the short story; but midway through the second episode the narrative is transformed into an extended fantasy that stretches far beyond Puttermesser's self-sustaining illusion of Uncle Zindel. And narrative transformation becomes itself the harbinger of more profound transformations at the heart of the novella. Here as elsewhere in Ozick fantasy becomes a mode of discovery, its various permutations clarifying the very reality from which it departs. Reality for Puttermesser adds up to the sum of her losses: of her majestic Bronx apartment, her only "home"; of sixty percent of the bones beneath her gums to periodontal disease; of her married lover, Morris Rappoport; finally of her Civil Service job in the Municipal Building. Now forty-six, Puttermesser "knew she would never marry, but she was not yet reconciled to childlessness. Sometimes the thought that she would never give birth tore her heart" (91). This greatest loss of all is symptomatic of the aridity of her personal—and professional—life. Her beloved former apartment ravaged by arsonists, her gums by periodontal disease, her sex life by Rappoport's defection, her professional life first by demotion then by firing, Puttermesser leads an increasingly constricted and barren existence. The reduced circumstances of her daily life are symbolized by the new "luxury" apartment she hates: cramped and airless, it is a far cry from the "Alhambra spaciousness" of her former apartment in the Bronx.

Yet Puttermesser's intellectual life remains undiminished. Ever the insatiable reader, she loses Rappoport when she insists on finishing the last thirty-three pages of Plato's *Theaetetus* before making love. Significantly, Puttermesser has just read about Thales, the ancient Greek philosopher, stumbling into a well while contemplating the stars. Like Thales and unlike Rappoport, Puttermesser is bemused by the big philosophical questions, especially those concerned with the "powers and properties" which "distinguish human nature from any other." And Puttermesser retains her belief—once manifest in her dream of Uncle Zindel—in the "uses of fantasy" as a means of self-definition. Just as these very habits of mind made credible the dream of Uncle Zindel, so they lend psychological plausibility to the far more extravagant fantasy that surfaces in the novella's crucial second episode. In Puttermesser's bed lies a naked girl looking dead, all white and bloodless. Moments before, Puttermesser, distraught at her own childlessness, had imagined the daughter she would never have—and the child's death. Thus the mysterious girl is Puttermesser's surrogate daughter just as Uncle Zindel was her surrogate father/mentor. But Zindel's unreality was blatant, the girl's nature conjectural. Coated with reddish powder, so pliable that Puttermesser's "correcting hand" can alter her features, shocked into life by Puttermesser's uttering the Hebrew Name of Names, the girl is apparently the first female golem. A creature fashioned from clay—all of the pots containing Puttermesser's plants are cracked, "vandalized," their earth "stolen"— the golem is a familiar figure in Jewish folklore. Artificial human beings, golems beg the very questions about human nature that, according to Socrates, Thales pondered in the *Theaetetus* (Ozick's golem rejects Leah, the name Puttermesser always imagined for her daughter, instead naming herself Xanthippe after Socrates' shrewish wife). Traditionally forbidden to speak, the golem writes: "Here you spoke the Name of the Giver of Life. You blew in my nostril and encouraged my soul. You circled my clay seven times. You enveloped me with your spirit. You pronounced the Name and brought me to myself. Therefore I call you mother" (97). Puttermesser, omnivorous reader that she is, recognizes this as one of the many golem-making formulas stemming from the Kabbalah (medieval mystical texts interpreting the Torah). And she had all but memorized "The Idea of the Golem," Gershom Scholem's classic essay on the subject.

For Ozick, "Gershom Scholem is a historian who has remade the world," a scholar who "went in pursuit of the cosmos." In her tribute to Scholem ("The Fourth Sparrow: The Magisterial Reach of Gershom Scholem") Ozick

lauds him above all for "his reclamation of Kabbalah."⁵
An important aspect of Scholem's work, abundantly evident in "The Idea of the Golem," is its demonstration of the profound seriousness at the heart of the Kabbalah's mysteries. Even the golem—easily dismissed by "rationalists" as a figment of Jewish hysteria, superstition, paranoia—is an aspect of the Kabbalah's grounding "in a belief in divine disclosure and the irrepressible hope of redemption."⁶ A kabbalistic commentary on Genesis, for example, posits an Adam created by God from earth. A man who creates a golem (Puttermesser and Xanthippe seem to be female firsts) therefore competes with God.⁷ Making a golem would seem to parody God's creative power, reducing divine disclosure to a kind of parlor trick. And a thirteenth-century text warns specifically against creating "another man, lest the world succumb to idolatry." One should therefore study such phenomena as golem-making "only in order to know the omnipotence of the Creator of this world," cautioned the prophet Jeremiah, "but not in order really to practice them."⁸ That Xanthippe is neither consciously conceived nor fashioned may absolve Puttermesser from the sins of idolatry and idol-making so abhorred by Ozick and condemned by the Jewish tradition.

Nevertheless, Jewish feelings about golems are ambiguous. Although a golem is potentially as much an idol as is a golden calf, the impulse that created it and the uses to which it is put may be far removed from idolatry. Attempting to emulate God is not necessarily attempting to rival God, and the form of worship it suggests may not necessarily violate the Second Commandment. This idea that the act of golem-making, not the golem itself, is the locus of worship is evident in the "formula" for bringing a golem to life. Puttermesser's uttering aloud one of the ''Names of the Creator'' over the hitherto inanimate lump in her bed and thereby shocking it into life may be read as an affirmation of God's power, not an exercise of her own. Scholem recalls the legend of the twelfth-century French Talmudist who created a golem for ''no other purpose than to demonstrate the power of the holy Name.'' No sooner is the golem created than it is ''dissolved again into dust,'' having served its purpose, which is purely psychic.[9] In Puttermesser's case the ''demonstration'' has its psychic origins not only in the same reverence for the holy Name that inspired Scholem's medieval Talmudist but perhaps at least equally in her subconscious—and impossible—wish for progeny. That Puttermesser at forty-six ''conceives'' Xanthippe is itself a ''demonstration,'' a visible embodiment of her hitherto unfulfilled motherhood miraculously conferred by God. In a purely Jewish context the golem's appearance to Puttermesser could even be a symbolic reaffirmation of the covenant between God and His chosen people. Nor does this interpretation necessarily foreclose the ''realistic'' one: that the entire golem episode that dominates the novella is a product of the same Puttermesser dreaming that once invoked Uncle Zindel.

Xanthippe springs from Puttermesser's dreaming of daughters but also of an ideal Civil Service and of New York converted into an earthly paradise. Deriving in good part from her own Kafkaesque demotion and dismissal from public service, Puttermesser's vision of New York reformed expands Xanthippe's role from that of surrogate daughter and personal servant to that of social redeemer. Because a golem's actions can only reflect its maker's intelligence, Puttermesser's messianic yearnings are evident in Xanthippe's program for New York. Created mayor by

her increasingly large and powerful golem, Puttermesser
presides over a "city of seraphim" where youth gangs,
muggers, thieves, and addicts work together for the general welfare. New York, turned into a *gan eydn,* a paradise on earth, represents civilization reborn. Puttermesser
sees in the city's transformation not primarily the creation
of the new but the recovery of the old: New York is "re-
suscitated," "reformed," "reinvigorated," and, especially, "redeemed." This vocabulary of change—like the
nature of the golem who brings it about—is symptomatic
of Jewish dreams of renewal. The centuries-old kabbalistic
theory of the golem as Adam reborn expresses Jewish
yearnings for and anxieties about continuity, yearnings
and anxieties rendered more desperate than ever by the
Holocaust.

Yet at the heart of Puttermesser's scheme of civic reha-
bilitation lies its contradiction: Paradise cannot be attained
on earth. Still, the immediate agent of destruction is the
golem, whose sexual rampaging unravels the social fabric
she wove together. Xanthippe's feverish but ultimately
sterile sexuality is an exaggerated representation of the affinity between a golem and its creator. A golem cannot
procreate; neither can Puttermesser. Yet they share the
longing for daughters that can never be. Appropriating
Rappoport, Puttermesser's erstwhile lover, for herself, the
golem again blurs the distinction between creator and created. Xanthippe's erotic adventures and frequent absences
not only evince a desire for a life of her own but threaten
to reverse the theoretically inalterable relationship with
her maker. Made to serve, the golem has instead gone her
own way, wreaking havoc on New York, destroying
Mayor Puttermesser's reputation, and effectively converting her maker into the golem's golem. So close has been

Puttermesser's identification with her creation, however, that in destroying Xanthippe—"O my mother, mother of my life!" pleads the dying golem—she destroys a part of herself. "O lost New York! . . . O lost Xanthippe!" cries Puttermesser, her dream of a better world as dead as her dream of daughters. The death of her dreams presages, if not her own end, then at least its imminence. Having undergone periodontal surgery, Puttermesser is left "unendingly conscious of her own skeleton." Intermittently masked by the novella's comic surface is the terrible bleakness of its final vision: of humanity unfulfilled, of society unredeemed.

In the Puttermesser stories, as in "Levitation," feminine identity is explored but largely subsumed into contexts which are first and foremost Jewish. Ruth Puttermesser and Lucy Feingold are women whose personal identities are enmeshed with and largely fashioned by their Jewish identities, whatever those may be. But in "Shots" Ozick's obsession with Jewish themes is restricted to a general, and by no means exclusively Jewish, emphasis on remembering—and preserving—history. Lacking specifically Jewish concerns, "Shots" focuses instead on the sexual and artistic identities of its first-person narrator—a female photographer involved in a love affair with a married man. Narrative method and anonymity (she remains nameless throughout the story) lend the photographer individuality and representiveness respectively. The narrator's love affair with Sam, more intense but no less hopeless than Puttermesser's with Rappoport, evokes identical premonitions of the future: "I am already thirty-six years old, tomorrow I will be forty-eight years old" (56). Compressed into a single sentence, those twelve years, like the twelve that elapse between the two Puttermesser stories, foreclose the dream of marriage and children. Because the love affair in ''Shots'' is central, Puttermesser's peripheral, the loss of a potential husband seems no less devastating to the photographer than the fear of childlessness. In any event, her camera is a stand-in for marriage and children just as Puttermesser's golem was a surrogate daughter. And just as the presence of the golem raised questions about the practice of Judaism, so the presence of the camera raises questions about the practice of art. ''Shots'' is a parable of the artist but of an artist who also happens to be a woman.

Elsewhere Ozick has distinguished between fable and the ''low form'' of allegory: ''In an allegory, the story *stands for* an idea, and the idea can be isolated entirely apart from the story; in a parable, story and idea are so inextricably fused that they cannot be torn free of each other.''[10] Thus in ''Shots'' ideas about the nature and function of photography are crucial to the narrator's identity. This interpenetration of life and art is most startlingly symbolized at a political symposium when the photographer/narrator ''shoots'' a speaker at the precise instant of his assassination ''and was amazed to see blood spring out of a hole in his neck.'' While the simultaneous shots of the camerawoman and the killer stress the connection between a particular art and the reality it records, Ozick's parable of the artist is not confined to the photographer. The narrator's fascination with death and time might as easily be expressed through literature, for example. And the analogy between photography and the plastic arts is made explicit by the narrator's comparison of ''time as stasis'' in a photograph with ''the time . . . of Keats's Grecian urn.'' What is more important than the artist's medium is the artist's talent and dedication. In ''Shots'' the photographer is uninterested in technical matters although she is "a close-mouthed professional, serious about my trade" (41). The story's first sentence: "I came to photography as I came to infatuation—with no special talent for it, and with no point of view," establishes the symbolic interchangeability of art forms as well as the link between the narrator's art (photography) and her love affair with Sam (infatuation), the chief concerns of her life.

At the heart of Ozick's treatment of the relationship between life and art lies an interest in how they illuminate each other. The Feingolds in "Levitation" are both literary hacks; but the fact that she writes about domestic life, he about Jews, adumbrates their essential incompatibility most evident in his levitating above her at the end of the story. In her 1976 essay "Justice (Again) to Edith Wharton," Ozick invokes the famous photograph of the writer seated at a desk to launch an interpretation of Wharton as artist and woman. Yet the formal "posed" Wharton, the lady of fashion ensconced in an ornate chair before a clean desk, is a far cry from the Wharton who actually composed her works on a writing board, in bed. While the photograph may not actually lie, it must be read in the light not only of what it reveals but of what it conceals.

If it is true, as Susan Sontag maintains, that "people robbed of their past seem to make the most fervent picture takers," then the camerawoman of "Shots," though not overtly Jewish, is emblematically so.[11] "Dead faces" draw her to photography. She experiences an epiphany of sorts in the form of a discarded photo which she finds "in a corner of the yard behind the Home for the Elderly Female Ill." In the "Brown Girl" of the photo the future camerawoman perceives the decaying old-lady-to-be and laments the impossibility of arresting her in the prime of life. The narrator imagines the Brown Girl—fading with the approach of death—exactly as she imagines herself at the end of "Shots." Trying on a period dress, she becomes the Brown Girl, and in a replay of her adolescent epiphany envisions her own dissolution and death. That Sam will remain with his wife (the aptly named Verity) is certified by photographing them side by side. This photo of the couple, framed in their daughter's mirror and fated to "stick forever," evokes the dimensions of the photographer's loss. She is left in possession only of her camera, "my ambassador of desire, my secret house with its single shutter, my chaste aperture, my dead infant, husband of my bosom." Like the Puttermesser stories, "Shots" limns the exigencies of feminine identity and culminates in a shattering epiphany of loss. Indeed, the camerawoman is abundantly aware of playing the cliché-ridden role of the "other woman" in love with a man who complains endlessly about his wife yet will never leave her. But the constant interpenetration of life and art reflected in the narrator's self-concept and the story's imagery suggests that "Shots" is better read as a parable of the female artist than of the female lover.

Any implication that women are fulfilled only as wives and mothers is, of course, anathema to feminists, Ozick included. Unlike many feminists, however, Ozick disdains such classifications as "woman writer," arguing vehemently against what she calls the "Ovarian Theory of Literature."[12] To see in the sex of the artist the key to the work of art is invariably to classify the art of women as somehow different from and most likely inferior to that of men. Although the art versus life parable in "Shots" features a woman artist, it would be equally valid for her male counterpart. The photographer/narrator, dedicated to her art, is finally unfulfilled as a woman. Yet the more profound lesson of ''Shots'' is that art and life are inseparable. That Sam and Verity will ''stick forever'' in her photo validates her art no less than their marriage: both are ways of living.

The photographer's camera, Puttermesser's golem, the Feingolds' novels—like the stories in which they are encased—represent art. And art, for Ozick, is as often destructive as creative. Always it smacks of that idolatry which violates the strictures of the Second Commandment. Unchecked—and often unwittingly—the creative impulse may result in a kind of blasphemy of the imagination. At its most horrifyingly aberrant the runaway imagination produced the Holocaust—''the burnt offering of the Jewish people in the furnace of the German Moloch.''[13] It is Ozick's—and Judaism's—deep fear of the irrational that is most evident in ''Freud's Room,'' the first of the two fragments ''From a Refugee's Notebook.'' As in ''Shots'' and ''Justice (Again) to Edith Wharton,'' an unusually evocative photograph becomes a mode of discovery. A series of famous photographs of Freud in the rooms where he wrote his treatises and analyzed his patients strikes the refugee/diarist as particularly revelatory. What is most striking—and most disturbing—to the writer is the proliferation of the ''ancient stone animals and carved figurines'' which Freud collected: ''Especially the gods. The gods, the gods!'' (60).

Ozick's distaste for Freud may owe as much to his rupture with the old as to his espousal of the new: postulating a secular demonology, he displaces the God of his fathers. The refugee's aversion to Freud is likewise shaped by the

Second Commandment's proscription against graven images. "The Sewing Harem," the second fragment "From a Refugee's Notebook," may be read as an antimodern diatribe. Lacking any apparent connection with the refugee, its putative author, "The Sewing Harem" is a Swiftian satire in the form of a parable. Ozick directs her barbs against the sexually and technologically sophisticated society—recognizably our own—of the planet Acirema (America spelled backwards) where, children being no longer welcome, the women sew up their vaginas. Still, occasional births result: stitches are clandestinely snipped during the periods when the women rent themselves out to rich businessmen. These accidental and unwanted children, who represent "the most regressive forces on the planet," interrupt the "personal development" and interfere with the "most profound ideals" of their mothers. The latter half of the story focuses upon the outcast offspring—"an ugly, anxious, stern-minded crew"—who band together in sects. Their idol, a superior goddess whose totems—stone vulvae—eventually cover the entire planet, is a sad and perverted reinvention of motherhood. Here Ozick's attack on idolatry is subsumed under her broader attack on the breakdown of traditional values—family, children—that begets false gods.

"Metaphor and irony are, worked together, very nearly art's everything" for Ozick.[14] The sewn vaginas and stone vulvae of "The Sewing Harem" function as powerful metaphors for a society whose selfishness and sterility spawn barbarity and chaos. Ironically, it is the exaggeration of modern ideals of sexual freedom and personal growth that engender a new primitivism. In her Phi Beta Kappa address at Harvard (1985) Ozick stressed the vital importance of metaphor in tracing this decline from a state of apparent civilization to one of "barbarism and savagery." "The Sewing Harem" is

> a parable. Also a satire, outfitted in drollery and ribaldry. Drenched, above all, in metaphor. The tale of a lascivious planet too earnestly self-important to tolerate children could only have been directed against artifice and malice, sophistry and self-indulgence; it could only have pressed for fruitfulness and health, sanity and generosity, bloom and continuity. My story and its barren conclusion were, I thought, a contrivance that declared itself on the side of life.[15]

The life-affirming message of "The Sewing Harem" must, however, be extrapolated from its life-denying context. For here, as in much of *Levitation: Five Fictions,* the imagery of death endlessly threatens to crush the metaphors of life. Such metaphors, couched in darkness, seem not to define Ozick's reality so much as desperately to defend against it.

NOTES

1. Ozick, *Levitation: Five Fictions* (New York: Knopf, 1982) 12. Page references in parentheses are to this edition.

2. Victor Strandberg, "Ozick, Cynthia," *Contemporary Novelists, 4th ed.,* ed. D. L. Kirkpatrick (New York: St. Martin's, 1986) 658.

3. Richard Bernstein, "On Being Nice or Rotten in Writing," *The New York Times* Living Arts, 3 Oct. 1989: 13.

4. Ozick, *Art and Ardor* (New York: Knopf, 1983) 139.

5. *Art and Ardor* 138–50.

6. *Art and Ardor* 140.

7. Gershom G. Scholem, "The Idea of the Golem," *On the Kabbalah and Its Symbolism,* trans. Ralph Manheim (New York: Schocken, 1965) 159.

8. Scholem 179–81.

9. Scholem 190.

10. Catherine Rainwater and William J. Scheick, ''An Interview with Cynthia Ozick (Summer 1982),'' *Texas Studies in Language and Literature* 25 (Summer 1983) 262–263.

11. Susan Sontag, *On Photography* (New York: Dell, 1977) 10.

12. *Art and Ardor* 266.

13. *Art and Ardor* 236.

14. Rainwater and Scheick 263.

15. Ozick, *Metaphor and Memory* (New York: Knopf, 1989) 267.

CHAPTER SIX

The Cannibal Galaxy, The Messiah of Stockholm

Cannibalism—personal, literary, cultural, cosmic—is the dominant force in Ozick's second novel, *The Cannibal Galaxy* (1983). Seemingly driven by an instinct as inexorable as it is universal, characters symbolically devour, or attempt to devour, each other. In so doing, they unconsciously replicate the modus operandi of the cosmic order, of "those megalosaurian colonies of primordial gases that devour smaller brother-galaxies."[1] So expansive is Ozick's controlling metaphor that it accounts not only for the central mystery of creation in the grandiose spectacle of galactic interplay, but equally for the no less elusive mystery of human creativity. At the heart of the metaphor lies a paradox: that cannibalism creates as well as destroys. Moreover, creation and destruction may be simultaneous as well as interdependent, as in the action of a cannibal galaxy.

Joseph Brill, the main character of *The Cannibal Galaxy*, understands cannibalism solely in its destructive aspect. A Holocaust survivor who witnessed the Nazi cannibalization of his family, of his fellow Jews, and of his native France, Brill holds an understandably bleak view of humanity. The wartime years of hiding, first in the cellar of a convent school, later in a hayloft, rob Brill of his youth and skew his intellect. Once an aspiring astronomer, Brill in late middle age is a primary school principal whose motto, *ad astra,* is an ironic footnote to his diminution. As Principal Brill, he has translated reaching for the stars into founding a school "of the middle and in the middle" which, like its creator, "had a horror of coasts and margins; of edges and extremes of any sort" (3).

The Edmond Fleg Primary School is the joint product of his Jewish heritage and French culture, the former transmitted by his father and Rabbi Pult, the latter by Paris and the library of an eccentric priest which Brill devoured in his cellar hiding place. Like Edmond Fleg, né Flegenheimer, Parisian dandy and fervent Jew, Brill had a vision of uniting modern European and traditional Jewish cultures. The Dual Curriculum that results is a dilution rather than a synthesis of the two cultures. Its failure is spotlighted at a commencement exercise when Brill's lofty educational philosophizing is belied by the mindless mishmash of Hebrew, English, and French sung by the fifthgrade choir. Teachers are disciplinarians or timeservers, turning out mediocrities whose academic "success" has been predicted by Dr. Glypost, the school psychologist, on the basis of a battery of tests designed to separate the worthless from the worthwhile.

On one level *The Cannibal Galaxy* can be read as a satire on American education in all its emptiness. But Ozick's barbs are launched not so much at the system as at its progenitor. For the emptiness of the Dual Curriculum results from the emptiness of Joseph Brill. Brill's is a failure of imagination symptomized by his postwar abandonment of astronomy and subsequent flight to America. Submerged in the American Midwest, Brill symbolically recapitulates his wartime existence. His apartment at the Fleg School is, ironically, a converted hayloft. It is as if Brill's spiritual and intellectual development were arrested in the original hayloft. Ostensibly a visionary ideal, the Dual Curriculum is actually a misguided effort to patch together the shattered fragments of Brill's youth. Just as the hope implicit in conceiving the Dual Curriculum characterized the young Joseph, so the hopelessness of its actualization characterizes Principal Brill. In late middle age he has given up serious reading and has exchanged his subscription of *Le Monde* for the banality of the local paper. Evenings are passed dozing or stupefied before the television set.

A worst-case philosophical scenario even implicates Brill in the destruction of the very Jewish culture which the Dual Curriculum was designed to preserve. For Ozick, who believes that "when a Jew becomes a secular person he is no longer a Jew" and that "nothing thought or written in Diaspora has ever been able to last unless it has been centrally Jewish," Brill's brainchild is a contradiction in terms.[2] Inevitably the Jewish half of the Dual Curriculum would vanish into the maw of Western culture. By unwittingly laying the pedagogical groundwork for the cannibalization of Jewish culture, Brill has aligned himself not with Judaism's preservers but with its destroyers. The bland sameness of the students at the Edmond Fleg Primary School is the end product of the Dual Curriculum. Such cultural homogenization is the precursor of the assimilation that Ozick dreads. Proclaiming their resemblance to others, denying their uniqueness as a people, assimilated Jews ensure "the obliteration of our progeny."[3]

But Ozick's indictment of Joseph Brill contains a more serious charge than that of abetting an act of cultural cannibalism. Principal Brill, who sees himself as a man of "almost sacral power," has created an idol in the Dual Curriculum. Idolatry, a recurrent theme and something of a bête noire in Ozick's essays and fiction, is for Jews the primal affront to God. In an essay in which she accuses critic Harold Bloom of fashioning an idol of literature, Ozick defines the idol-maker as one who "envies the Creator, hopes to compete with the Creator, and schemes to invent a substitute for the Creator."[4]

Even as a boy growing up in a traditional Jewish home in Paris, Brill was enticed by idols. One day, daring to enter the Musée Carnavalet, Joseph is struck by the beauty of a statue and simultaneously astounded that this object of Gentile homage is Rachel the Mother of Israel. That night he relates his adventure to his mother, who "instantly saw his trouble—she knew what a museum signified. A pagan hall had enticed him, an image had ensnared him." Ignoring his protest that the stone beauty was, after all, Rachel, and warning him to "keep away from such a sty," his mother closes the discussion: "An image is an image" (9). But later at the university young Brill alters his diction and every night scours the fish smell from his father's shop off his hands, actions that symbolically distance him from his Jewish heritage. Drinking in Western Civilization and immersing himself in Latin, he grows enraptured with French literature—"the nuances of Verlaine maddened him with idolatrous joy" (12). Only when Joseph begins to grasp the essentially anti-Semitic nature of the culture he venerates does he abandon literature and history. He decides "to learn the cold, cold skies" of astronomy because "he was sick of human adventure'' (16). Yet his prewar choice of astronomy, like his postwar decision to bury himself in the American heartland where ''nothing ever happened,'' symbolizes a flight not from idolatry but from life. As safe as it is sterile, Brill's idol—the Dual Curriculum—is the fitting embodiment of the bleak world view of its creator.

Despite the outward success of the Edmond Fleg Primary School, Principal Brill recognizes its mediocrity—as he recognizes his own. Musing on the likeness of ''Fleg'' to phlegmatic and to ''Phlegethon, the river of fire that runs through Hell,'' Brill imagines himself a man of middling age and abilities, set down in the middle of ''an ashen America,'' and beset by hordes of middling teachers, students, and parents. Brill's personal life occupies the same middle ground as his Dual Curriculum and is just as hopeless. Aging and unmarried, lacking progeny and even friends, Brill is himself representative of the emptiness he sees everywhere. He seems consciously to have shaped his life to conform to his own blighted perception of human nature and human destiny. Conceivably, Brill's pessimism is a variant of his idol-making and equally offensive in the eyes of God. If the idolater would displace God the Creator, the misanthrope would prejudge God's creation.

It is at the exact point in *The Cannibal Galaxy* when Brill is most downcast at the prospect of eternal sameness—''Nature replaces, replaces identically, replaces chillingly'' (45)—that Hester Lilt and her daughter Beulah enter the novel. Hester Lilt is, like Brill, a product of European culture, but there the resemblance ends. Brill winces at Hester's ''I've become what I intended to be''; he, the would-be astronomer, clearly has not. Hester, a

The Cannibal Galaxy

self-styled "imagistic linguistic logician," is a high-powered intellectual, as uncompromisingly honest as she is formidably erudite. To the awed Brill, whose long-dormant imagination she momentarily awakens, her omnivorous intelligence is like a cannibal galaxy that devours its smaller brethren. It is Hester who devastatingly summarizes the man Brill has become—or has failed to become. Dismissing his argument for abandoning astronomy—"For me it was the heights or nothing"—Hester replies, "You stopped too soon" (63). Assuming himself incapable of scaling the heights, Brill foreclosed his future, an act of self-cannibalization ironically opposed to the creative cannibalism of Hester or the ogre-galaxy.

The crux of Hester Lilt's lesson about stopping too soon is contained in her "eccentric lecture on Theory of Education." She tells the story of the little fox scampering across the "barren and desolate" place where the Temple stood before its destruction. To Rabbi Akiva's "Why do you weep?" his three colleagues reply that the place formerly occupied by the Holy of Holies is now the domain of the fox. Then Akiva explains to the three why he laughs:

'Because of the prophecy of Uriah and because of the prophecy of Zechariah. Uriah said, "Zion shall be ploughed as a field, and Jerusalem shall become heaps." Zechariah said, "Yet again shall the streets of Jerusalem be filled with boys and girls playing." 'So you see,' said Rabbi Akiva, 'now that Uriah's prophecy has been fulfilled, it is certain that Zechariah's prophecy will also be fulfilled' (68).

The error of Akiva's fellow rabbis—and of Brill—is to stop too soon, surrendering not only the present but the future to the fox, taking "the fox and all its qualities to be right, proper, and permanent." The centrality of the parable grows even more apparent in light of the fact that *The Cannibal Galaxy* began life as a short story called "The Laughter of Akiva" (*The New Yorker* 10 Nov. 1980), incidentally a sort of literary cannibalization by which the smaller work is ingested to spawn the larger. In *The Cannibal Galaxy* the diametrically opposed outlooks of Akiva and the other three rabbis are dramatized by Hester Lilt and Joseph Brill respectively. Hester's endlessly probing intelligence works "to make a frame for every idea." Hers is the dream of creating new life from the void: "Her ambition, her desire, was to cast molds, to bring form into being" (63–64). For Brill, the void is all. His creation—endless recapitulation of existent mediocrity—admits of few surprises, much less miracles. Unable to share Hester's hope, Brill is nonetheless able to recognize her intellectual vitality.

It is Brill's admiration for Hester Lilt that inspires him to admit her daughter, Beulah, to the Fleg School despite an unfavorable psychological evaluation by Dr. Glypost, whose standard tests label Beulah a "non-achiever." Dr. Glypost is a cruder version of Brill in her simplistic confidence about predicting the future. Yet despite Dr. Glypost's—and his own—view that nothing changes, Brill imagines that Hester's brilliance must be reflected, however dimly, in her child. For eight years he watches Beulah, vainly looking for some sign of her mother in the silent and dreamy daughter. All the while Brill oscillates between pride—that Beulah's ordinariness confirms his theory of unchanging mediocrity—and despair—that Hester's daughter, of all children, cannot prove the exception to the rule. As if trying to fathom the mystery of a

The Cannibal Galaxy

creation that produces a mother and child so unlike, Brill talks compulsively to Hester on the telephone. He first decides that Hester lacks normal maternal instincts, and that her own brilliance blinds her to Beulah's shortcomings. Later, at a birthday party for Beulah, he discovers that Hester is nothing but maternal, and that for her "only Beulah mattered." To Brill's remark that Beulah is "nothing," Hester replies, "She's everything. She's my life" (92). Where Brill sees only a poor student, a "little crippled creature," Hester sees unlimited potential: "She's going to be original." Brill concludes that "Beulah had made her mother mad" (100–01).

The revelation that Hester Lilt as mother is no different from other women in her love for, and delusions about, her child liberates Brill from her intellectual dominance. When Beulah graduates from the Edmond Fleg Primary School, apparently as ordinary as when she entered, he takes it as proof of his hypothesis that nothing changes. That Beulah conforms less to her mother's dreams than to Dr. Glypost's psychological profile seems to invalidate Hester's—and Rabbi Akiva's—philosophy. At the same time, given his belief in "nature's prank of duplication," Brill is grieved that eight years of the closest scrutiny have uncovered no trace of the mother in the daughter. Granted that mediocrity is inalterable, how is the very fact of mediocrity in the child of such a mother to be explained? It is, of course, the impossibility of explanation that interests Ozick.

Confident that he knows all there is to know about Beulah, Brill believes he has "decoded" Hester as well. In a last telephone conversation with Hester, Brill accuses her of feeding on Beulah, of converting her daughter's nothingness into a philosophical tool. Thus the principle of not stopping too soon becomes a justification of Beulah, and Hester's entire philosophy is designed "to make things fit what she is." Without Beulah, there is no Hester:

> You *need* her! You need her to be nothing, so you can be something. She's Genesis Chapter One, Verse Two—*tohu vavohu,* unformed and void, darkness over the deep, so you can spin out your Creation from her! . . . Look how you use, you eat, you cannibalize your own child! (115).

As usual, Brill takes the part for the whole, seeing in Hester's cannibalism only an intellectual conceit and failing to appreciate its power to create in a fuller sense.

Although *The Cannibal Galaxy* is a novel of ideas, its structure corresponds less to the evolution of Brill's thought than to stages of his involvement in life. The novel falls roughly into three parts: Brill alone; Brill and the Lilts; Brill as husband and father. Because he is a principal and his school is the novel's main locale, the divisions of *The Cannibal Galaxy* generally reflect those of the school year. The middle, and most important, part of the novel thus opens with Hester enrolling Beulah at the start of a new term and closes eight years later with Beulah's graduation and the end of Brill's direct involvement with the Lilts. And it is shortly before commencement that Brill reveals his marriage plans to Hester during their last telephone conversation.

Brill breaks the news of his forthcoming marriage only moments before his telephone assault on Hester. Whether the attack is provoked by Hester's scoffing reference to Iris, Brill's office clerk and wife-to-be, or by his new-found confidence in his ability to decipher Hester, the end of the phone call marks the beginning of Brill's new life:

"And after that Brill's life went quickly, quickly" (115). Years fly by in the last one-third of *The Cannibal Galaxy*. It is as if Brill's triumphant denunciation of Hester frees him from her influence—and from the pressure to think as well. Momentarily jolted from his intellectual torpor by Hester's probing brilliance, Brill quickly lapses back into his former state. With the relentlessly ordinary yet loudly demanding Iris, Brill acts out a comically accelerated parody of conventional bourgeois marriage. Already in his sixties when he marries a woman half his age, Brill quickly fathers a son, Naphtali.

When Naphtali shows signs of brilliance, it seems tempting to read *The Cannibal Galaxy* as one of those novels of redemption in which the wayward hero rights himself in the end by embracing "life." Such a reading elevates ordinary life (family, home, television), once despised by Brill, to the summum bonum. Brill, who feared not only his own ordinariness but its reproduction, comes to realize his affinity with his fellow human beings, and gains in his waning years the courage to be husband and father. And as a bonus this belated son shows signs of incipient genius. Naphtali's intellectual precociousness, unstinting curiosity, and straight-A schoolwork ease Brill's fears that his presumed genetic mediocrity will pass on to his offspring. Although he shifted gears relatively late in life, Brill seems finally to have profited from Hester Lilt's oft-repeated injunction not to stop too soon.

Redemption for Ozick does not, however, consist in exchanging one brand of mediocrity for another. Nor does it consist in erecting new idols in place of old. Thus Brill's new life comes no closer to reaching for the stars (*ad astra*) than did his former one. Not only does his relationship with Iris decline into boredom and petty bickering, but Naphtali turns out to be only middling, a business administration major at Miami U. Naphtali's ironic apotheosis from child prodigy to business major explodes Brill's latest idol. Ozick's debunking of Naphtali is reminiscent of her ironic deflation of an earlier idol—the Dual Curriculum. The Brill who sinks into the lethargy and bitterness of old age remains visibly unredeemed, his idols shattered, his understanding clouded.

Naphtali's near-comic metamorphosis is paired with a far more startling transformation—that of silent and backward Beulah Lilt into avant-garde painter, articulate, brilliant, darling of the art world. It is the sight of Beulah being interviewed on a television talk show that destroys the last vestige of Brill's certitude. So meaningless was the Dual Curriculum for Beulah that she can recall no detail of her primary school for the television interviewer. Taken together with Naphtali's conspicuous success in the same course of study, Beulah's dismissal of her early education powerfully suggests that prodigies do not arise from the Dual Curriculum but despite it. And it is no accident that Beulah speaks from France, she and Hester having reversed the course of Brill's postwar flight to the United States.

The sudden reversal at the end of *The Cannibal Galaxy* when Beulah becomes a genius, Naphtali a nonentity, is as outrageous as it is arbitrary. And therein lies the meaning of the novel. Forgetting the Second Commandment, Brill has worshiped false idols (Dual Curriculum, Naphtali) whose downfall is his punishment: "Beulah Lilt's language assailed him endlessly. It oppressed him. She had forgotten her childhood in the Curriculum that was his treasure and his name, as dear to him as his son Naphtali'' (162). Ultimately *The Cannibal Galaxy* is an argument against interpretation. Denizens of a creation as mysterious as it is limitless, human beings interpret at their own peril. Near the end of *The Cannibal Galaxy* Brill, still unable to fathom the miracle of Beulah Lilt, is struck by the illumination in her once-dead eyes: "Who," he wonders, "had polished those green stones?" (149). The answer lies no more in nature than in nurture. For Ozick, the only polisher is God.

The Messiah of Stockholm

The Messiah of Stockholm (1987), like *The Cannibal Galaxy,* features an obsessive hero and revolves about the mystery of creation. Again the limits of probability are approached, occasionally breached. The device of sudden reversal by which backward Beulah Lilt is apotheosized into exciting avant-garde artist at the end of *The Cannibal Galaxy* is itself reversed in *The Messiah of Stockholm.* Here the "miracle," the central improbability that drives the narrative, is proposed at the outset. Lars Andemening, the main character of *The Messiah of Stockholm,* puts his faith in the sort of outrageous possibility that Joseph Brill would have rejected out of hand. Yet Andemening, the willing believer, suffers a loss of faith, while Brill, the man of little faith, is forced by the undeniable reality of the transformed Beulah Lilt into a semblance of grudging belief.

It is Andemening's initial belief—obsession—that he is the son of Bruno Schulz, the Jewish Polish writer shot dead in the street of his native Drohobycz by an S. S. agent in 1942. Schulz, who earned his living as a high school art teacher, first gained literary recognition at the age of forty with a collection of stories published under the title *Cinnamon Shops* (known as *The Street of Crocodiles* in the U.S.) in 1934. Three years later he published his second, and final, collection of prose fiction—*Sanatorium under the Sign of the Hourglass.* Rumor had it that he was working on a novel called *The Messiah* (hence Ozick's title) at the time of his death. An offshoot of the same rumor had a friend of Schulz's hiding the manuscript which, in any event, has never been found. In an epigraph to *The Messiah of Stockholm,* Ozick quotes Schulz on the infinity of forms, a notion dear to her own heart and abundantly evident in *The Cannibal Galaxy.* Endlessly mutating and renewing, species will continue to multiply even should the "recipes" of the Creator be lost. For "even if the classical methods of creation should prove inaccessible for evermore, there still remain some illegal methods, an infinity of heretical and criminal methods."[5]

So vital is the creative principle for Schulz that no "dead matter" exists. Only tenuous and tentative boundaries separate the animate from the inanimate: Trees "stood with their arms upraised, like witnesses of terrifying visions, and screamed and screamed."[6] Paper birds rise into the air, tailor's dummies are "half-organic, . . . the result of a fantastic fermentation of matter."[7] In the "dense darkness" of the "wild and spacious" night of a typical Schulz story, formlessness is the rule rather than the exception. Objects swirl through the air, their everyday solidity melting into the stuff of dream—or nightmare. At the center of this intensely private world stands the father, " 'that incorrigible improviser" launching a counteroffensive against the suffocating and pervasive boredom of provincial Drohobycz, defending "the lost cause of poetry.' " A Drohobycz merchant who ran a textile business until forced by illness to retire into "ten years of enforced idleness and his own world of dreams," the father slowly cedes bits and pieces of his identity, drifting ever further away from the human community. Eddying helplessly within a delusional system of his own making, he is terrifyingly and endlessly metamorphosed, finally assuming the form of the creature he most loathes—a cockroach.

To Ozick such "phantasmagoric transfiguration" powerfully characterizes the writing of Slavic Jews—Franz Kafka, Isaac Babel, Isaac Bashevis Singer, Jerzy Kosinski. They and the characters they so hauntingly portray are marginal men, existing provisionally at the fringes of Central or East Europe. All reflect the same "homelessness and ultimate pariahship felt by Schulz," none more poignantly than Kafka, whose affinity with Schulz is most obvious. Schulz, who translated *The Trial* into Polish, abundantly shares Kafka's father obsession and metamorphic fantasies. In Schulz's Drohobycz, ominously called Crocodile Street, "nothing succeeds, . . . nothing can ever reach a definite conclusion."[8] This visionary setting is forever dissolving and re-forming, perhaps mirroring outwardly the inward turmoil that shuttles the father between hallucinatory nights and relatively stable days. That Ozick is drawn to the Slavic Jewish writers—coreligionists, literary precursors—is evident in much of her work, nowhere more so than in *The Messiah of Stockholm*. Its hypothesis—the conceivable existence of a lost manuscript and, less conceivably, of an unknown son of Bruno Schulz—superimposes 1930s Drohobycz onto 1980s Stockholm. These juxtapositions—Jews and Gentiles, past and present, East and West—prefigure the complications and ambiguities of Lars Andemening's identity crisis. Few writers mine the enigmas of identity more relentlessly or profoundly than Franz Kafka, whose framed likeness presides over Ozick's study (*New York Times Book Review* 10 Sept. 1989). *The Messiah of Stockholm* is dedicated to Philip Roth, whose obsessions with Jewish identity (transparently his own) are postmodern versions of Kafka's. E. J. Lonoff, the writer-recluse of Roth's *The Ghost Writer*, is a latter-day Kafka—or Schulz—whose hero is "a nobody from nowhere, away from a home where he is not missed, yet to which he must return without delay." And Amy Bellette, in the same novel, is a concentration camp survivor whose conviction that she is Anne Frank is as apparently outrageous as Lars Andemening's belief that he is the son of Bruno Schulz.

Grounded in the fictions of Schulz and, by extension, in those of Kafka, Lars Andemening's father obsession inevitably reflects its origins. In both Schulz and Kafka the father looms large in the son's imagination. Whether the father is potent (Kafka) or feeble (Schulz) the influence of his presence is unremitting. The apparently disparate metamorphic fantasies wherein the son (Kafka) and the father (Schulz) become bugs share a common source: father obsession. Lars Andemening—spare, twice-divorced, forty-two-year old once-a-week book reviewer—believes that he has been derailed from his destiny, that he belongs elsewhere, in short that he is the son of Bruno Schulz. So positive is Andemening that he was in his mother's womb that day over forty years ago when his "father" was gunned down in an obscure Galician town that he becomes proficient in Polish. Compulsively he reads and rereads Schulz's tales until, consumed by their texts, he feels himself caught in an undertow, drowning in the miasma of mind that envelopes the typical Schulz story. Lars senses affinities in looks, in voice, in mind between himself and the dead father whose "murdered eye" periodically regards him. And Ozick, provisionally reincarnating Schulz in Lars Andemening, fashions *The Messiah of Stockholm* into a Schulz-like tale of father obsession and metamorphic fantasies. She may additionally be slyly underlining the affinities between Schulz's work and her own when she has Lars refer to an American review of *The Street of Crocodiles.* Ozick wrote just such a review, itself perhaps the genesis of *The Messiah of Stockholm.* [9] Indeed the novel is in part about the taking over, the devouring, the usurpation of another's text—a recurring Ozick theme. Appropriating Schulz's fictional world, she recapitulates a cosmos as antic as it is mysterious. As Lars enters deeper and deeper into the phantasmagoria of the mind invoked by Schulz and reinvoked by Ozick, his father obsession grows ever more plausible. As an orphan he has the "terrifying" freedom to choose his own identity. The role he elects to play, incredible in the real world, is lent whatever credence it possesses by Schulz's theory of infinite forms and nuances quoted in Ozick's epigraph to *The Messiah of Stockholm.*

A son's search for his real—or symbolic—father is as old as literature itself. In its archetypal treatment in Homer's *Odyssey* the search is for a real (biological) father. In *Ulysses,* James Joyce's modern rendering of the *Odyssey,* the uncongenial relationship between real father and son provokes Stephen Dedalus's search for a spiritual father. And in *Trust,* Ozick's unnamed narrator must first learn her father's identity in order to certify her own and to confront him as his daughter. Whatever the exact nature of the relationship between father and child, the search culminates logically in a recognition scene. But in *The Messiah of Stockholm* no such recognition scene is possible: Bruno Schulz is undeniably dead, and Lars Andemening's search is conducted not among men but among manuscripts. That the father's existence is only textual demarcates *The Messiah of Stockholm* from traditional quest literature. Post-Holocaust quests in the works of Jewish writers occasionally culminate in the miraculous reunification of families or friends, but far more often become their own epitaphs. As such, they exist as textual surrogates for the millions of Jewish victims and thereby serve as tokens of remembrance. What lends poignancy to Lars's necessarily textual father obsession is its paradigmatic quality: In the wake of the Holocaust, Jewish yearning can find no other form.

Lars's search for every scrap of paper by or about Bruno Schulz is largely carried out at Heidi Eklund's bookstore. Herself a refugee, the round, sixty-five-year-old German woman becomes Lars's confidante, and together they sift through the pathetically meager stock of letters and photographs relating to Schulz. Heidi also plays devil's advocate, arguing that if *The Messiah* is lost it has no existence, that what "matters is what's here to be read." She is equally skeptical about Lars's claim to be Schulz's son, a claim that has no more basis in fact than does the missing manuscript. An unrelenting realist, Heidi forces Lars again and again to confront the central fact about Schulz—his murder—and dismisses as madness Lars's undocumented intuitions. For Heidi, there is a "smoldering cultishness" in Lars's worship of Schulz as father. Indeed, like Joseph Brill in *The Cannibal Galaxy,* Lars is guilty of idolatry. And in Lars's case the object of adulation is a dead man who can be revered only in bits and scraps of paper. Thus Lars's obsession with texts, with following any paper trail no matter how faint that leads to or from the necessary father.

Were it not for its residue of truth, Lars's father obsession would be merely pathetic. That truth lies in Schulz's—and Ozick's—belief in the infinitude of forms, in the notion that reality is as thin as the paper Lars chases. The "creative recipes" of Schulz's Demiurge—cited in the epigraph to *The Messiah of Stockholm*—may produce hitherto undreamed of permutations, such as the metamorphosis of Beulah Lilt in *The Cannibal Galaxy*. Some such theory of universal plenitude seems at first to explain the mysterious appearance of a woman who not only calls herself Schulz's daughter but claims to be carrying around the original manuscript of *The Messiah* in her little white plastic bag. Lars's reaction to Heidi's news of his "sister" is as comic as it is ironic. His instinctive reflex to deny the identity of the sister causes him simultaneously to deny the authenticity of the very manuscript whose imagined existence had been the centerpiece of his father obsession. Yet if Schulz might have fathered a son, why not a daughter? And if *The Messiah* had been written and lost, why might it not be recovered? Willing, even compelled, to attribute his own identity as Schulz's son to the mysteries inherent in creation, Lars shrinks from imagining equally arbitrary geometries that might account for an unknown daughter and a lost manuscript.

Adela's claim—that she is Schulz's daughter by one of his high school art students—has, of course, no more or less factual authenticity than does Lars's. Still, at their first meeting Lars accuses her of appropriating her name—and thus her identity—from Schulz's *The Street of Crocodiles* and *Sanatorium under the Sign of the*

Hourglass. In both fictions Adela is "the blue-eyed, temperamental, young servant girl, . . . the household acolyte, the disturbing, sex-charged element"[10] whose vitality contrasts sharply with the bland insubstantiality of the mother. Amidst the endlessly dissolving dreamscapes of Schulz's fiction, the earthy and matter-of-fact Adela is singularly stable. In *The Street of Crocodiles* Adela's substantiality underscores the dilemma of the father, "condemned to float eternally on the periphery of life, in half-real regions, on the margins of existence." The father's marginality is attributed by the narrator son to the mother's indifference: " 'She had never loved him' " I thought, " 'and as father had not been rooted in any woman's heart, he could not merge with any reality.' "[11] Lars Andemening's instinctive hostility toward the self-proclaimed daughter who calls herself Adela may signal the understandable fear of a twice-divorced man who, like the fictional father, has no roots in a woman's heart, and whose life in Stockholm is as provisional and peripheral as was the father's in Drohobycz. This latter-day Adela threatens to displace, even shred, the fragile identity that Lars has so painstakingly assembled, much as her fictional counterpart dominated the father. In "Father's Last Escape," the final episode of *Sanatorium under the Sign of the Hourglass,* it is no accident that Adela's departure for America and consequently the beginning of a new age—"empty, sober, and joyless, like a sheet of white paper"—coincides with the father's death. Although the father's shuttling between life and death is a favorite Schulz leitmotif, this time he is "definitely dead," perhaps as a direct consequence of his final severance from Adela, the life principle, the embodiment of reality. The crumpling of the world into a "sheet of white paper" is the fitting climax to *Sanatorium under the Sign of the Hourglass,* a fiction whose first episode, "The Book," signaled its persistent "textuality." Of course it is this same dependence upon the vagaries of texts, themselves (like the manuscript of *The Messiah*) conjectural, unreliable, that once sustained Lars but now threatens to overwhelm him. Adela's arrival with a life story and a lost manuscript— "texts" that clash with Lars's—turns *The Messiah of Stockholm* momentarily into a mystery novel. What is her true identity? Is the manuscript authentic? When Adela appears at his flat with the account of her birth and the lengthy and complicated tale of how *The Messiah* fell into her hands and asks him to translate the manuscript into Swedish, Lars is torn between reflexive denial and the compulsion to know the truth. The ensuing struggle over Adela's white purse and her escape with the still unexamined manuscript prolong mysteries and postpone revelations. But the most profound effect of the inconclusive encounter is the change wrought in Lars. Like the metamorphosed subjects of Schulz's fictions, Lars is transformed overnight from a mesmerized explorer of the thorny texts of Central Europeans (Broch, Canetti, Kundera) to a facile reviewer of popular fiction, and from a son whose father's (Schulz's) scrutinizing eye conferred identity to one newly orphaned by the withdrawal of that confirming gaze. Prefigured in his failed attempt to seize *The Messiah* from Adela is the even greater loss of the relationship Lars had fashioned with the manuscript's author. Once the leading actor in a self-fashioned drama, Lars is reduced to a bit player in an action contrived by others.

Those others—Adela, Heidi, principally the elusive Dr. Eklund—may or may not be engaged in a conspiracy to palm off a phony manuscript of *The Messiah*. All may be playing roles: Adela, the innocent bearer of the recovered manuscript; Heidi, her usual devil's advocate, questioning its authenticity; and Dr. Eklund, the scholarly authority who will pass ultimate judgment on the text. No sooner does Dr. Eklund pronounce the manuscript to be the genuine *Messiah* than Lars falls savagely upon the text, ravaging its pages for the presence of his erstwhile father so recently denied. What he finds is Schulz's familiar Drohobycz universe, but a universe emptied of people and inhabited only by idols. Lacking human beings to worship them, the idols start to bow to one another, then to sacrifice to one another. As the more powerful idols cast the weaker ones into the sacrificial flames, the acrid smoke of roasting metal settles over Drohobycz. Only at this point does the Messiah arrive, a Messiah (notes Lars) who resembles a book. In fact the Messiah seems to be The Book—the enigmatic symbol of creation in all its beauty, abundance, potential—a ''splendiferous thing'' which ''exceeds all our capacity for wonder'' and dominates Schulz's first episode of *Sanatorium under the Sign of the Hourglass*. Just prior to its own collapse, the Messiah gives birth to a bird which dissolves the idols into sparks, leaving Drohobycz desolate: ''The human beings—gone; the idols—gone; only this small beating bird born of an organism called the Messiah, and dim wails dying . . . '' (111).

The transmogrified world of the manuscript's last pages is Ozick's terrifying redaction of Schulz's habitual dreamscape. Holocaust imagery fuses the works and days of Ozick and Schulz into a seamless—and somber—account of the wages of idolatry. The small bird destroys the idols with a ''tiny wand of hay''—a sliver from a mammoth bundle in the cellar of the Drohobycz synagogue, where it was slept on by a saintly Jew called Moses the Righteous One. Whether or not the bird represents the purging flame of true religion, it further links Schulz's texts—with their many birds—to those moments in *The Messiah of Stockholm* when Lars dreams of birds in conjunction with his father's eye. But whatever the bird's precise meaning or function in the manuscript, it serves in *The Messiah of Stockholm* primarily to spotlight Ozick's recurring theme of idolatry and its consequences.

Following the "animal urgency" of Lars's reading—itself a form of idol worship—Adela, Heidi, and Dr. Eklund urge him to use his Monday column to announce the existence of *The Messiah*. Dr. Eklund actually uses the word "annunciation," and Heidi adds that *The Messiah* exists only if people believe in it. To Lars, their choice of words amounts to a deification of the text: "That sounds like God" (115). Moreover, their words echo one another's as if they were rehearsed speeches in a preordained scenario. So polished is their performance that the possibility of conspiracy is invoked: Could this be the climax of a complicated and sophisticated plot to foist upon Lars—and the public—a literary forgery? Thus conceived, Act 1 featured Heidi's downplaying of Lars's claims while simultaneously feeding them; Act 2 the "miraculous" appearance of Adela with the "miraculously" recovered manuscript of *The Messiah;* and Act 3 the equally fortuitous return of the hitherto mysterious and missing Dr. Eklund just in the nick of time to pronounce the manuscript authentic.

Whatever the exact nature of the "conspiracy," it invokes Ozick's theme of idolatry. Believing the manuscript to be a forgery authored by Dr. Eklund, Lars sees *The*

Messiah as a false idol erected by the conspirators: "You want to be in competition with God" (128). Of course Lars himself is a co-conspirator in the sense that out of his dreams and delusions sprang the original idol, the manuscript's progenitor. Lars's burning of the manuscript represents therefore not only the destruction of the blasphemous forgery of those who would compete with God but also a form of personal atonement for his own role in its genesis. Read as a relatively straightforward account of the birth, sustenance, and eventual death of idols, *The Messiah of Stockholm* becomes an object lesson on observing the strictures of the Second Commandment. Lars Andemening comes across as a man whose wanderings through the Schulz-like byways of the imagination culminate in a more realistic vision of the self, a vision symbolized by the "fitful eyeglasses" that he wears some seven months after burning the manuscript. The new Lars, in the process of "robotizing himself," has jettisoned the indecipherable Central European writers, sticking to simple Swedes and Americans. No longer boyish, gaining weight, immersed not in his past illusions but in the routine of the office, Lars soon becomes the *Morgontörn's* star reviewer.

Yet Lars's assumption of a "normal" life begs the same questions that Ozick raised about Joseph Brill late in *The Cannibal Galaxy*. Like Brill, Lars seems nearly anesthetized, drained of the visionary capacity that may exalt as well as delude. That Lars requires his new reading glasses to write even one paragraph evidences a symbolic nearsightedness that no glasses will correct. The ambiguity of Lars's new identity is the subject of the final two chapters of *The Messiah of Stockholm*. And the symbolism of sight is again employed in its investigation: Lars can no longer visualize the eye that appeared to him in the fullness of his belief in Schulz the father. The missing eye—which only belief can summon—is itself emblematic of Lars's lost faith. Whether a vestige of that faith remains is tested by the reappearance of Adela, now calling herself Elsa Vaz. Admitting that she is Dr. Eklund's daughter and that Lars was being used by the conspirators, she nonetheless insists upon the authenticity of *The Messiah,* employing terms such as "cremated" and "annihilated" to describe Lars's destruction of the manuscript. Her powerfully condemnatory words—more often reserved for the horrors of the Holocaust than for the burning of books—constitute a devastating indictment of Lars. For if the manuscript was Schulz's lost *Messiah,* then Lars has reenacted in its burning the destruction of a people and a past. And *The Messiah of Stockholm,* far from being an endorsement of normalcy attained, becomes instead a cautionary tale of normalcy purchased at too great a price.

Following the departure of Elsa Vaz, Lars occasionally finds himself believing her story. As infrequent as the onset of belief are the moments when he "grieved for his life." Still he is haunted by the "smell of something roasting," a lingering reminder of the Holocaust imagery invoked by Elsa Vaz. With time the smell recedes, afflicting Lars less and less often with its companion vision of a last Drohobycz scene in which a man in the long black coat of an East European Jew hurries toward the chimneys "with a metal garter box squeezed under his arm" (144). That box and its presumed contents—the manuscript of Bruno Schulz's *Messiah,* now forever lost—trigger Lars's sporadic bouts of grief. It is perhaps only at such rare moments that the robotized Lars is fleetingly reanimated by a capacity for belief, a capacity, Ozick seems to suggest, which renders us most fully human.

NOTES

1. Ozick, *The Cannibal Galaxy* (New York: Knopf, 1983) 69. Page references in parentheses are to this edition.

2. Ozick, *Art and Ardor* (New York: Knopf, 1983) 168–69.

3. *Art and Ardor* 168.

4. *Art and Ardor* 195.

5. Ozick, *The Messiah of Stockholm* (New York: Knopf, 1987). Page references in parentheses are to this edition.

6. Bruno Schulz, *The Street of Crocodiles,* trans. Celia Wieniewska (New York: Walker, 1963) 114.

7. *Street of Crocodiles* 57.

8. *Art and Ardor* 227.

9. *The New York Times Book Review* 13 Feb. 1977; rpt. *Art and Ardor* 224–28.

10. Schulz, *Sanatorium under the Sign of the Hourglass,* trans. Celia Wieniewska (London: Picador, 1980), translator's preface xii.

11. *Street of Crocodiles* 107.

BIBLIOGRAPHY

Works by Cynthia Ozick

Trust. New York: New American Library, 1966; London: MacGibbon and Kee, 1967. Novel.

The Pagan Rabbi and Other Stories. New York: Knopf, 1971; London: Secker and Warburg, 1972.

Bloodshed and Three Novellas. New York: Knopf, 1976; London: Secker and Warburg, 1976.

Levitation: Five Fictions. New York: Knopf, 1982; London: Secker and Warburg, 1982. Stories.

The Cannibal Galaxy. New York: Knopf, 1983; London: Secker and Warburg, 1983. Novel.

Art and Ardor. New York: Knopf, 1983. Essays.

The Messiah of Stockholm. New York: Knopf, 1987; London: Secker and Warburg, 1987. Novel.

Metaphor and Memory. New York: Knopf, 1989. Essays.

The Shawl. New York: Knopf, 1989. Stories.

Critical Works about Ozick

BIBLIOGRAPHY

Currier, Susan, and Daniel J. Cahill. "A Bibliography of Writings by Cynthia Ozick." *Texas Studies in Literature and Language* 25 (Summer 1983): 313–21.

Bibliography

BOOKS

Bloom, Harold, ed. *Modern Critical Views: Cynthia Ozick.* New York: Chelsea House, 1986. The nineteen articles, many of them brief reviews, deal mainly with single texts but also with recurring motifs in Ozick's work. The Knopp, Rosenberg, and Strandberg articles cited below are reprinted.

Pinsker, Sanford. *The Uncompromising Fictions of Cynthia Ozick.* Columbia: University of Missouri Press, 1987. This brief chronological survey emphasizes the way Ozick's work redefines Jewish American writing by stressing its essential Jewishness.

ARTICLES AND PARTS OF BOOKS

Chertok, Haim. "Ozick's Hoofprints." *Yiddish* 6.4 (1987): 5–12. Focusing chiefly on *Levitation: Five Fictions,* Chertok concludes that "no other writer . . . has dealt as explicitly with this chronic crisis [paganism vs. Judaism] in the Jewish soul."

Cohen, Sarah Blacher, Ed. "The Jewish Literary Comediennes." *Comic Relief: Humor in Contemporary American Literature.* Urbana: University of Illinois Press, 1978. 172–86. Unlike some Jewish writers who exploit ethnic externals for easy laughs, Ozick is a "comedienne of ideas" who "transforms the farcical into the philosophical."

Cole, Diane, "Cynthia Ozick." *Twentieth-Century American-Jewish Fiction Writers.* Ed. Daniel Walden. Vol. 28, Dictionary of Literary Biography. Detroit: Gale Research, 1984. 213–25. This critical survey of Ozick's work is especially valuable for its treatment of *Trust.*

Epstein, Joseph. "Cynthia Ozick, Jewish Writer." *Commentary* Mar. 1984: 64–69. Ozick's essays are more to be admired than her often "fantastical" fiction. Those stories "written in a more realistic mode" are among her best.

Harap, Louis. "The Religious Art of Cynthia Ozick." *Judaism* 33 (1984): 353–63. Ozick's "commitment to a pervasive Jewish spirit" is traced in selected stories from her first two collections.

Hellerstein, Kathryn. "Yiddish Voices in American English." *The State of the Language.* Ed. Leonard Michaels and Christopher Ricks, Berkeley: University of California Press, 1979. 182–201. In "Envy; or, Yiddish in America" Ozick makes English sound like Yiddish "by transposing Yiddish syntax into her prose."

Bibliography

Knopp, Josephine Z. "The Jewish Stories of Cynthia Ozick." *Studies in American Jewish Literature* 1 (1975): 31–38. The fictions in *The Pagan Rabbi and Other Stories* display Ozick's "acute historical consciousness, an understanding of the role of Judaism in world history."

Rosenberg, Ruth. "Covenanted to the Law." *MELUS: The Journal of the Society for the Study of the Multi-Ethnic Literature of the United States* 9 (1982): 39–44. A close reading of "Usurpation" reveals that Ozick's "narrative constitutes itself as impassioned literary criticism."

Strandberg, Victor. "The Art of Cynthia Ozick." *Texas Studies in Literature and Language* 25 (Summer 1983): 266–312. This perceptive critical survey of Ozick's fiction defines her crucial issues as Jewish identity, the seductiveness of Hellenism, and the relationship between fiction and reality.

INTERVIEWS

Bernstein, Richard. "On Being Nice or Rotten in Writing." *The New York Times* 3 Oct. 1989: 13–14.

Ottenberg, Eve. "The Rich Visions of Cynthia Ozick." *The New York Times Magazine* 10 Apr. 1983: 47, 62–66.

Rainwater, Catherine, and William J. Scheick. "An Interview with Cynthia Ozick (Summer 1982)." *Texas Studies in Literature and Language* 25 (Summer 1983): 255–65.

Index

The index does not include references to material in the notes.

Index

Index

Index